99 Blogging Tips, Strategies And Must Haves

Make Your Blog A Success

By: Mick Macro

Mick Macro

Preface to 99 Blogging Tips, Strategies, And Must-Haves

Hello, and welcome to my big book of blogging tips.

In my first book, 99 Ways To Flood Your Website With Traffic, I showed you all of the different ways of getting traffic to your website or blog, both paid and free, organic, viral, online, offline.

In that book, it was all about traffic, and that is what a lot of you got. It feels good to have helped quite a few people get those first 1,000s of hits to their site. And then when you combine different strategies to make your own great big traffic strategy (tailored to YOU), it makes things easy to automate, easy to grow, and eventually easy to get traffic whenever you want.

This book is all about the BLOG.

This book will take you through the necessities and commonalities that all successful blogs need and share. You will learn tips, strategies, must-haves, and really just a detailed look at all of the things you should be thinking about when creating a blog. This book covers some traffic and promotion strategies, a lot of tools and blog necessities, the type of content you SHOULD be creating, monetizing your blog, creating a product (or two, or three!), and a lot of other little "gold nuggets" as some of us say. There are very basic tips and strategies (especially at the start), but there are also some more advanced strategies later in the book.

But don't get me wrong, this book isn't for everyone. I was recently checking out my book reviews for my first book, and although the positives out-weigh the negatives, there were still a few 'hate' reviews. But guess what? That's okay, because those people weren't right for the book. One person said the book was useless, that "most of these stuffs won't get you any traffic", yet the book has continued to help people get traffic to their websites and blogs to this day. Another reviewer tried to claim that the only thing I said in my last book was to "promote your website to get better website traffic". However, there were 98 more strategies he missed, plus an extra bonus, and about 170 pages of content.

And another said they were "probably just too old to appreciate the book", which makes me quite sad. There's no age limit on website traffic. Same goes for blogs. It doesn't come down to age, gender, race, religion, or anything like that. It all comes down to hard work, and daily consistent action.

If you don't know how to do something, learn how to do it. If you meet a roadblock, don't focus on the problem, focus on the solution. Do everything in your power to get past the roadblocks, and eventually something that was hard will become easy. And then more challenges and sticky situations will arise. But you have to break right through them. You will break right through them.

So please, take this book seriously, and really take a look at all 99 chapters. You might think you've "been there, done that", but I guarantee you there is always something you can do to make your blog more successful, and that is what I hope to do right now in this book.

Don't look at this book as an "I need to use every single strategy exactly as it is written", instead look at this book as an "If my blog needs help in this area, this is one way to get the job done". This book is just a huge arsenal of blogging tips and strategies that you can use to make you and your blog more successful.

Thanks for reading the preface.

Now let's get started.

Mick Macro

1

THE 3 W QUESTIONS

Before we get into any advanced strategies and blogging tips, it's important to have a strong foundation. These first few chapters will cover that foundation, and then you'll move on to strategies, advanced tips, monetization, blog products, etc.

I believe the first thing you need to do before even creating the blog is ask yourself 3 questions. I call them the Ws. Who are you? Why should people listen to you? What do you have to offer? Let's dive in a little deeper...

Who are you?

Seriously, who are you? What's your name, what is your background, what country are you from?

Tell your readers who you are, and what you're about. Your blog readers will be more likely to come back, because they get that personal feeling. The feeling that they are visiting your blog to visit YOU. Make the social blogging experience more friendly, which will indeed grab the attention of more people.

Why should people listen to you?

You don't have to directly tell people why they should listen to you, it should be transparent from the very beginning.

Telling your readers who you are is great, but now you have to put your money where your mouth is. People listen to people with great content. People listen to people who are helpful. People listen to people who are inspiring and positive.

When someone visits your blog, what are the first few things they see? Does your blog make you look like a reliable, trustworthy, personable source? These are just some things to think about, we'll get into more strategic thinking later.

What do you have to offer?

Here we are, the offer. What do you have to offer to your visitors? If I sent you 10,000 visitors to your blog, do they convert? Do they opt-in to an email list? Do they share your content for you? Do they buy a product? Do they download a freebie?

But it's not just about getting the leads - it's about giving them an offer they can't refuse. Again, I'll get into a lot more detail on these strategies later in this book, but these are the things you need to be thinking about BEFORE anything else. You can get all the traffic in the world to a page on your blog, but if you don't have something to offer, then all of that traffic goes to waste.

2

Defining Your Mission And Goals

Okay, so you've gone through the three Ws, now it's time to define your mission and your goals.

It doesn't matter where you put it, just make sure it's on your blog and people can find it easily. Some have it on their 'about me' page, some have it on their home page. Others put it in their header at the top of every page.

Defining your mission should be easy. Why did you make your blog? Is it to help people, entertain people, inform people?

Explain in one sentence what people can expect from your blog. For example: "JacksVeryCoolWebsite.com is dedicated to helping young entrepreneurs reach their goals through the power of hard work and action."

People have the "what's in it for me?" mentality. When someone visits your blog, they want to know what it is you're bringing to the table. How is your blog different from the others? Why should I come back, what's in it for me in the future?

If you fail to establish your mission, the passerbyers will just be passerbyers. However, if you establish what you can do for them now AND in the future, the passerbyers will become subscribers, then members, then buyers. All of that... starts with a clear mission.

So what about goals?

Your goals are for yourself, but they are just as important as establishing your mission.

If you want 100,000 visitors a month, that's an awesome goal to have! Depending on how hard you work, and how smart you work, it might take awhile - but that's okay! Just having the goal in your mind will make it that much more beneficial to work hard on the blogging strategies that are proven to work, because then you know you'll reach your goals, and may in fact pass them.

Okay, ready to really get started?

Who are you, why should people listen to you, what do you have to offer, establish your mission, define your goals - that's the very core foundation of your blog, your business, and you.

The next part of this book will go into detail about all of the tools, plug-ins, and other things that every blog needs. After that, I'll introduce some strategies to push your blog to the top, and finally you'll learn some advanced strategies. There's a lot to uncover in this book, enjoy.

3

Domain Name

If you already have a domain name for your blog, feel free to skip this chapter (same goes for the next tip about blogging services). However, I would recommend you to at least skim through it, you may pick up an extra tip or two.

Your domain name is just another important piece of the blog puzzle. It's hard to say what the single most important aspect of a blog is, but your domain name (ex: yoursite.com) is up their at the top of the list.

People remember domain names. Remember, this is the NAME OF YOUR BLOG. If it's a personal blog, buy your name - FirstnameLastname.com - trust me, it will be GONE before you know it.

If it's your business name, get your business name. If you are starting a new blog that isn't personal and isn't for any specific business (yet), you need to be creative these days.

Having your main niche keyword in your blog name is good for SEO. Like PetIguanaMaster.com - I didn't even look that up. Not even sure if it exists yet. But if you were targeting pet iguana owners, or the keyword "pet iguana", then you just gave yourself a HUGE advantage over your competitors.

But if you don't want to go with keywords, then just make sure it is short and catchy.

It needs to have that special ring to it, the name that rolls off the tongue. Make it short, catchy, and try to include a keyword in there, and above all: make it easy on your readers to remember. Don't be the guy who has the blog that people talk about but don't know what it's called.

So where do you buy your domain name? There are literally thousands of sites selling domain names (probably 10s of thousands). There are big and small companies - I'd go with a big one. Just search "buy domain name", and look at the competition.

If you really want to make things easy on yourself, buy your hosting first, and buy it from a company who also sells domain names. This way, you can already have a running server, and once you buy the new domain name, it will be instantly added onto your server, with no hassle at all. I've used HostGator for just about everything, and I would give their 24/7 online chat support an A+, which is one of the biggest pitfalls of most other hosting services.

4

Blogging Service

Don't skip this chapter entirely if you think your answer is "Wordpress".

There are hundreds of different blogging platforms you can use, but you should only focus on a few. I didn't say 'one', I said 'a few'.

As you will find out in this book, there are many different types of blogs you should be thinking about creating.

Your main blog, the one that you pump and promote, should be on the most reliable, easiest, and advanced blogging platform. It should also work like a CMS, or content management system. Right now, the top choice (and in my opinion, the best) among most bloggers is Wordpress.

Wordpress makes it easy to setup a blog, a theme, a static website, images/audio/video, plug-ins, and all sorts of other great stuff. The possibilities are endless with Wordpress.

It doesn't stop there, though. I'll teach you about micro blogs and niche blogs and bait blogs and all sorts of other blogs. The point I want to make right now is that you don't want to put all your eggs in one basket.

Have your main blog on Wordpress, have a few niche blogs on Wordpress (but on a different server), have a handful of micro blogger blogs. Also think about the social blogs, like tumblr. There are actually people who have ONLY been to blogger blogs, who have ONLY been to Wordpress blogs, who have ONLY been to tumblr blogs. You'll find new audiences, new keywords, new links, and more success by having a few blog sites and systems in mind.

More on different types of blogs and what they can do for you later.

Whenever you use a new blogging platform, it's always important to test out all the featuers. Mess up a little bit in the testing stages. Don't be careful in the beginning.

Go ahead, make a mistake that makes your entire site not work. Then you can contact hosting support and have it fixed. What I'm saying is, it's better to have the problems at the very beginning than it is to have a big site issue a year from now, and the only reason it happened was because you were so careful for so long, and had never experienced something like this before.

This also allows you to test out different themes, find out how plug-ins are installed, find out what happens when you install a plug-in that says not compatible with your version of Wordpress. You can test images and thumbnails, categories and tags, colors and text, and 100s of more features.

You can switch between a 2-column theme and a 3-column theme, adjust sizes, add widgets to your sidebar - Just by messing around for a few hours with all the features makes it both easy and fun in the future whenever you work on your blog.

I'm sure you probably already have your favorite blogging service in mind, so for now, go with that one. Just have a small list of other popular blogging services, as you'll be using them later in this book.

5

HAVE A CATCHY TAGLINE

The tagline is sort of like your blog mission, but it can be more entertaining and less informative.

Although informative taglines are nice, you want something that stands out, you want your blog to be unique from the rest.

Ever notice the "just-made" Wordpress blogs, with the website name, then the tagline that says "Just another WordPress blog"? WordPress does that for a reason. They want you to change it to your own tagline (obviously) - However, most people just think for a minute, write down one of the first taglines that comes to their head, and moves on. WRONG MOVE.

The tagline is (or should be) one of the first things your visitors see when they arrive on your blog.

Here's an example of a bad tagline turned into a good headline:

BAD: "JacksUltimatelyCoolWebsite.com, the place for all your entertainment needs."
GOOD: "JacksUltimatelyCoolWebsite.com, Get Lost In The Coolness!"

BAD: "BuySomePinkUnderwear.com, where anyone can buy underwear."
GOOD: "BuySomePinkUnderwear.com, The Largest Collection Of Pink Underwear In The Universe."

Yeah yeah, those are just some 'off-the-top-of-my-head' examples, I'm sure you get the idea. If you have a blog already, take a look at your tagline. Say it 100 times. When people come to your blog, is your tagline really what you want people to see? Can you modify it in order to attract more people to your blog, and better yet, come back?

Another common mistake that bloggers make is they think they can only have one tagline. You don't. You can have as many as you want! Obviously, you can't show more than one tagline at once, but feel free to change around your tagline from time to time, and see how people react to it. If you find that you have a humorous audience, make your tagline funny. If you have an extremely serious audience that just wants the facts/tips/info, then make your tagline short, to-the-point, and informative.

It all depends on the type of blog you are running. That's why I started this book with the 3 Ws - so you are able to distinguish who you really are and what you are offering. Once you find out what you want to offer, and why people should listen to you, then the tagline (as well as a lot of other strategies) becomes easy.

6

RSS Feed Button and Submission

Okay, for the rest of the book, you will be introduced to tips, strategies, must-haves, and a lot of other great blogging gems.

These tips are in no official order, except for the fact that there are more in-depth strategies and tips later in the book. The book is laid out in a list-like format so that you can pick and choose what blog strategies and techniques you need to work on now, as well as combine together multiple strategies later for maximum leverage and success.

I thought it would be good to talk to you about RSS sooner rather than later. RSS stands for "Really Simple Syndication" (or "rich site summary", depending on how old school you are), and is basically a live feed of the content of your blog - usually just your blog posts.

You'll find that there are tons of different ways of getting people to come back to your blog, and your RSS feed is one of them.

You've seen RSS buttons all over the place - they are usually small orange buttons, and are frequently in the top right corner of blogs. This is because most blog themes use the top right corner as the default RSS feed button link location.

So first you need to make sure your RSS feed button (or link) displays on every page of your blog. Have a clear CTA (call to action) telling people to subscribe to your RSS feed, or just say "Subscribe To My Blog Here!".

The more visible your button or link, the more you'll find people subscribing to your feed. RSS works great because it is accessible by nearly every browser and computer - right now by clicking on the "feed" button of a random blog I found, it gives me the option to subscribe to the feed using: Live Bookmarks, Google Bookmarks, iWeb,

MyYahoo, and Safari. I'm sure there are more options and different options for you too.

WordPress makes RSS super easy, which it should. As soon as your blog is started on Wordpress, your RSS feed begins as well. Usually, your RSS feed URL will be YourSite. com/feed/, but is different for some. You can usually change your feed URL as well as use a service like FeedBurner to display your feed.

Besides having a feed, did you know you can SUBMIT your feed to RSS Feed Directories? It's sort of like a website directory, but specifically for blogs with content that updates all the time. There are thousands of feed directories, and it wouldn't be time effective to list them all out for you. Just do a search for "feed directories" or "rss feed submission", and you'll have 100 or more great feed submission sites to submit your feed to.

And instead of just having one link that shows up (like a website directory), some RSS feed directories keep track of your feed, and display feeds with recent posts first, and a lot of the time the most popular feeds (of the day/month/all time).

Once you have your blog feed URL submitted to a few hundred of these directories, you're SET. You don't have to keep submitting your articles, they just get updated as soon as you post them to your blog. These gives you a prime advantage over your competition, and you only have to set it up once per blog!

7

Pop-Up CTAs

Yeah, pop ups, but not the annoying ones!

Okay, maybe some people find them annoying, but I'm not talking about those old "you are our 1 zillionth visitor" popups. I'm talking about a clear call to action that tells your visitors to do something.

You're not just blogging for the hell of it, are you? Every blogger has goals, and one that remains constant among all bloggers is more traffic, more interaction, more people!

You want to get your blog visitors coming to your blog not just once, but multiple times! By the time they leave your blog, you want them to have done what you wanted them to do.

Maybe today it's "like me on facebook". Tomorrow it could be "follow me on twitter". The next day it could be "sign up for my email list and I'll give you a cookie".

Whatever you want your visitors to do, TELL THEM VIA POPUP. You can either decide to search through the WordPress plug-in directory to get a simple pop-up plug-in, or you could pay someone like "ActionPopUp" a small fee to have a fully customizable and unique pop-up function on your blog.

You can set your CTA to pop up right when they get to your site, 5 seconds after they get to your site, right before they leave, right when they leave, 5 minutes after they get to your site. You can choose to show it once per day per visitor, show all the time, only once per visit - the functionality is completely up to you.

The point is, make SURE you have some sort of CTA on your popup.

Sometimes people will browse around a blog for hours, and never sign up to their email list because they are so used to seeing email forms in the top right corner.

But when someone who gets to your site starts looking around, you can have a CTA show up saying "join my email list". If you decide to show your pop-up right before they leave your site, start your CTA with "Before you go..." - It gives people the feeling that their time on your blog isn't yet over. Whether or not they stay at that moment, you'll be getting many more opt-ins, leads, and can really tell your blog visitors to do whatever you want!

Another fun way of getting people to "do something" on your blog is to give away a free gift. More on that later.

8

SIDE BAR OPT-IN

This is the most common way of gathering people on a blog email list, and being able to e-mail them later.

The side bar opt-in form. You've seen them before, all successful blogs have e-mail lists and some sort of opt-in form.

You must stop thinking that it's all about driving brand new traffic to your blog all the time, and start thinking about how you are going to get them to come back.

Social media is a start - tell people to follow you on twitter, like you on facebook - that's fine. However, these people aren't as valuable as the people on your e-mail list, simply because people "like" hundreds and thousands of pages on facebook, they "follow" hundreds and thousands of twitter profiles. So when your message (tweet/update) goes out, it instantly gets buried underneath a thousand other updates from other people. With an email list, you are able to send an email out to your entire list, and actually have it be seen by almost everyone on the list! It doesn't matter how high or low your conversions are, I am positive that 1,000 email subscribers are better than 1,000 followers.

Followers and Likes and Fans means that someone has a vague interest in you. Subscribing to your email list means they trust you with their email privacy. Then, of course, when you send out great content to your list, they will eventually turn into leads, buyers, repeat buyers, repeat visitors, promoters, affiliates, partners - you name it, it can all start with a simple email opt-in form.

I again suggest using the 'big guys' - AWeber is my #1 choice, but there's also MailChimp, I believe ConstantContact, GetResponse. Of course, having an email list is going to cost you some money if you want it done right. You can usually get started for very little (AWeber has currently been running a "get started for $1" campaign forever), and then you pay for the email service monthly or yearly, and then you pay additional money depending on how big your email list is (how many subscribers you have). Yes, you have to pay for your subscribers. Don't worry, by the end of this book, you will find out how to optimize and monetize your e-mail list and your blog, so that you always profit.

Anyway, the sidebar opt-in form is one of the easiest things to do. You just pick a form, insert some text, add some other info like your e-mail you want to use (don't use free email services, use your domain email), and add the code to your sidebar. With WordPress blogs, you would simply drag and drop a "text" widget to your side bar, copy and paste the email opt-in form code, and save.

9

Splash Page Email Opt-In

Yes, these chapters are all about email and people opting in to become your lead.

I focus so much on opt-ins and leads simply because these are REPEAT visitors. Instead of having to promote each and every blog post to a slew of social media sites, you can instead just write an email, send it to your email subscribers, and watch the traffic come in.

In the last chapter, I went over email opt-in forms in the sidebar, and gave you a brief overview of how to get started with your own email list.

Although one email form is nice, it's not enough. Remember what I said before - EVERYONE has a sidebar email form? Well, that's exactly my point. EVERYONE is doing it. So, you need to not break away, but make additions. Go ahead and keep your sidebar opt-in, but then you should also create what most call a splash page.

This is usually a very short page, has one headline or tagline, maybe a few bullet points, and yep, you guessed it, an email opt-in form. Most people give an incentive that once they join/subscribe, they will instantly get some sort of free gift, ebook, etc. Also, most splash pages display without the need of a scroll bar. You shouldn't have to scroll down to see anything.

It's important to have a splash page for many reasons, the most important being that sometimes you don't want to send people to your blog. You see, even if you want someone to be a repeat visitor, you don't actually have to start with them on your blog. You can send traffic to your splash page, give them an offer they can't refuse, and then you are able to send them emails to go check out your blog later. And not just once, but multiple times - really as much as you want until they unsubscribe.

Also, if you ever plan on buying advertising in the future, or buy ads for your blog right now, you should NOT send the traffic to your blog. Instead, send them to your splash page, and offer them one free piece of content in exchange for their email address. It is much more valuable to you and your blog.

Let me put it this way:

A) You buy advertising and get 1,000 people to your blog. A majority of these people will be gone in less than 5 minutes, and will never return.

B) You buy advertising and get 1,000 people to your splash page. Let's say 50 of those people opt-in (5% opt-in rate is definitely doable on a splash page).

Now for both of those situations, let's say you publish 10 posts in the next month. With option A, you are unable to get those visitors back, and have to pay for future visitors. With option B, you have a ton of people you can send your articles to.

I know this chapter is about splash pages, I just thought it would be useful for you to understand a little more about the importance of email lists.

10

Opt-In Form Under Content

Okay, this is the last chapter about opt-in forms, and there's just one more (the next chapter) about a semi-advanced strategy about opt-ins and emails.

If you're reading this book from start to finish, and aren't skipping around, then you know the importance of the email list.

So you have an email form in your sidebar, an email form on your splash page - Why do you need an email form under your content?

It's simple really. It's all about maximizing your efforts, duplicating your results, and generally just making sure they see it! And what better time to ask someone to sign up for your email updates than right after they read a piece of great content from you?

Again, the process of getting an opt-in form under your content is going to be different for everyone. In WordPress, there are a few plug-ins (and themes) that allow you to insert any code before or after any section of your blog. You can put content above or below your header, above or below your footer, your blog posts, your sidebars, etc.

When you only have an email opt-in form in the top right corner of your blog, you aren't giving your readers enough time to generate a sense of trust with you. But, allow them to read your hopefully valuable content first, and right at that moment when they are overjoyed because of how much you helped them, you ask them to subscribe to your email updates for more [fill in the blank].

This is why having a blog in a specific niche is key. When you have a blog in a specific niche or micro niche, you are able to give your readers a more precise incentive for them to join your email list. If you were giving away a guide called "10 Steps To Being

More Productive", it would be easier to give it away on a blog all about productivity rather than self-help in general.

It's really a circular 3 step process: First you post/publish/upload valuable content to your blog, second you get people to visit your blog posts (the valuable content), and third you get them to join your email list.

There's just one more chapter about email and opting in, but this strategy is one that I hardly see anyone doing, so pay attention.

11

THE COMMENT OPT-IN CHECKBOX

I wouldn't classify this strategy as "new" or anything, but it's one that many overlook for one of two reasons: they either don't know how to do it, or they are too lazy to do it.

It's no secret that there are successful blogs using this strategy right now. Go check out a few of your favorite blogs and see if they are using it.

Want to know what to look for?

Underneath the content area (usually a simplel blog post), you should obviously have a comment section. Usually almost all comment plug-ins and default comment systems make the commenter enter a valid email address, their name, their website if they want to.

You can use this to your advantage. You are already "collecting" their information in order for them to comment, and even better - the information they provide to comment is all the info you need! Now, before they leave their comment, you ask them permission to add them to your email list.

You do this with a simple checkbox saying something like "Join our awesome club, too?".

I know some lightbulbs are turning on, but you might be thinking, Isn't this a little much? A little obtrusive?

Most of the time, no... in fact in my mind - it's not enough. You want to give yourself every chance in the world to land a new lead, and if you can increase your email subscribers by doing a one-time install of a little plug-in that basically collects email address of people interested in your content, I say why the hell aren't you doing it. So where do you find a plugin like this?

I'm postive you'll find something for free in the WordPress plug-in directory, but I suggest buying a professional plug-in, just because it will take the stress out of installing, setting up, making sure everything works, plus the additional support.

Right now I'm looking at a plug-in called "Optin Comments", and I'm sure you'll find dozens of similar plugins just by searching "opt in comments", "comments opt in", "opt in comments plugin".

You get the idea. Email lists are important. It gives you the chance to do so many things (which you'll learn in this book), like getting traffic, interaction, product sales, ebook downloads, affiliate commissions - the list goes on and on.

12

HAVE A SEARCH BAR ON YOUR BLOG

I'm happy to say that on most blogs I visit, they have a search bar. Bravo.

But some people are still missing out on the extra pageviews, repeat visitors, and new leads they could be getting. A search bar can prove to give your blog more interaction as well, but only if you understand when to really use a search bar.

I'll explain later in the book why having a lot of posts is important, but if you want a search bar on your blog, you better have a lot of posts. Nothing is worse than people searching for "web traffic" and not finding anything on your blog because you only have one article and you use the term "online traffic". When you have lots of posts, and tag them correctly, and include a lot of commonly searched keywords, it not only helps your SEO, but also helps people find what they are looking for.

And that's exactly why having a search bar is important - more interaction. People will find your blog, read a post, find it interesting, and maybe instead of them leaving, they'll search for a topic that they were scratching their head about earlier. When they find EXACTLY what they were searching for, they'll be more likely to comment, share, opt-in, and as you'll find out, BUY from you.

Some people say having a search bar on a blog with a low quantity of posts can hurt your blog, since people will search for something and not find it, and get frustrated and leave. Although I agree with that, I also think it really couldn't hurt, for two reasons. First, if you didn't have the search bar, they wouldn't search for anything in the first place. Having the search bar gives you an extra pageview (reduce bounce %), and gives you one more chance of turning that visitor into a commenter, repeat visitor, subscriber.

Also, some search bar plugins give you data on what people are searching for on your blog. If you find that people are searching for something a LOT but you don't have any posts about that yet, you can create a post about it, and enjoy the new flows of comments and interaction - because once again, your visitors will have found exactly what they were searching for.

13

Social Sharing Buttons

This should be a no brainer as well. This is not advanced. You can do this, and should.

The days are over where you post something on your blog and wait for the magic to happen. "Build it and they will come" doesn't work anymore. You now need to influence the interaction on your blog.

I don't care if it's just one "tweet" button, or one "facebook share" button, or even 20 different social sharing buttons - at least get something on your blog.

You can find hundreds of different free social buttons (and better paid ones) to add to your blog pages, blog posts, sales pages, splash pages, squeeze pages, etc.

Most bloggers find that just a handful of popular social sharing buttons works the best. It's really common sense - If you have too few social buttons, there may not be enough people that actually use that social service to share cool blogs. But then if you have too many, people will get irritated trying to finding the buttons (usually when 20 or 30 buttons are displayed at the same time, they are small icons that make it hard to read).

The social buttons you decide to use all depends on the type of blog you are running. Think about where you find content similar to your own. Is it Pinterest? Facebook? Twitter? Digg? Find the right combination of social service buttons to use, and you will find more sharing of your blog and more interaction on your blog.

14

Social Subscribe Buttons

Let me start off by telling you the difference between 'social sharing buttons' and 'social subscribe buttons'.

These aren't the only terms for these types of buttons, just what I and many others refer to them as. Social sharing buttons are for sharing your blog posts so that others will click over to your blog to read it too. Social subscribe buttons are buttons that allow people to follow you on twitter, like your page on facebook, share your entire blog on a blog ranking network.

Most social sites have some sort of plugin, widget, or code you can put on your blog to allow people to follow/like you. Sometimes you will have to just put an image link to your social profile and get people to follow or like or love you there.

Now, some people argue that the only thing these social subscribe buttons do is take people away from your blog. "You want people staying on your blog, not leaving to go to some social network", they say.

Sure they may be leaving your blog, but if they are that jumpy right now to where they go to a social network, like/follow my blog, and then don't come back, then they probably weren't ready to do much else on my blog anyway - So at least I got them one step further into future interaction.

Also, sometimes people just aren't ready to give you their email address and join your "cool list". However, they might be interested in following you on twitter, or liking you on facebook, and seeing what more you have to say.

Some people focus on now, but sometimes you have to think about the future.

15

Tags, Do They Help?

Tags, tags, tags. Tags are one of those things that almost everyone talks about, and I'm just another person talking about them. Or am I?

It's not that tags don't help, they just don't work like magic anymore.

In the "old days of the internet", you could tag a blog post with keywords like "6 pack abs", or "gardening tips", or "improve your golf swing", and within hours be on the first page of Google for that keyword.

And because it doesn't work this way anymore, many have concluded that tags are useless.

And here I am, talking about tags. So do they help?

They do help, but you can't look at tags as if they are going to boost your ranking for a specific keyword overnight.

Tags help when you do other SEO correctly. If you tag your post with "lose fat", "lose fat fast", "how to lose weight", and do nothing, then you won't get any special results. But then if you get 100 links pointing back to your website with those specific keywords, you'll find that your ranking will increase nicely.

Also, as I explained before, it helps to have tags when using a search bar plugin. Some search bars come with the functionality of being able to categorize by your tags, which means you can tag your post with "lose weight", "lose pounds", "lose 10 pounds", "weight loss", and tons of other tags, and have them be found when people search for them on your blog.

So yes, tags help a little with SEO, and a LOT with interaction, which is really what every blogger needs.

16

About Your Blog's Categories

Categories are more important than you think.

Categories are what distinguish what type types of posts you have, what type of person you are, and above all - what is in it for them.

I think it would be easiest to give you an example of what to do, and what NOT to do.

BAD Category Choices:

- Reviews of stuff
- Some thoughts
- Technology
- Websites
- Cool stuff
- Popular lists
- Tips and Strategies

GOOD Category Choices:

- Attracting leads and customers
- The technical side of online business
- Ultimate success strategies
- Short tips to improving your website
- Recommended sources and products
- Interviews of entrepreneurs

Of course, those examples are the ugly and the beautiful, and you are probably somewhere in between.

When you are choosing titles for your categories, you want to give your reader or visitor a sense of what you're about, what's in it for them - What will they learn, what will they gain?

And if you can't categorize like the "good" choices above, then you probably need to focus on less topics, and possibly start another blog for the other topics you blog about.

There's really only 2 steps to figuring out if a blog category works:

#1: Is it narrow enough so that people looking for one answer can find it in a variety of posts in that one category?

#2: Is it broad enough to the point of being able to write about new topics for that category for while?

Just figure out how many articles or pieces of content you will be able to produce in the future for a specific category, and if the answer is a high enough number for you to consider a lot of posts in a single category, then you have a winner.

17

Solid-Selling ABOUT Page

Don't overlook this. So many overlook their about page.

You've been to about pages before, it's what you click on to find out more about the blog.

Lots of about pages that I've seen simply include a couple notes about the blog, maybe a link to the home page, and sometimes a brief third-person bio of the owner of the blog.

You must think differently about your about page.

Your goal on this page should be to SELL. No, not sell products, sell yourself. You need to tell people who you are, what you are about, what results you have gotten, what others are saying about you, and why people need to be listening to your every word.

Don't just tell people you're a young entrepreneur from Idaho. Tell them you grew up poor, you started your own blog/business, you get these results, you do these things amazing, you can help people with this, you DO help people with this.

Be personal, and tell them why they should follow you, like you, add you, subscribe to you. You need to sell them on future interaction.

Don't let people leave your about page saying, "Cool guy." Make people leave your about page saying, "Wow, I'm going to subscribe to him/her and I can't wait to hear from him/her".

18

CONTACT PAGE (EMAIL VS FORM)

Every blog needs a contact page. Some people include contact forms or info on their about page, but as you just found out, you need a SELLING about page, not a "tell me your problems" page.

When people want to contact you, they want to interact. A contact page further increases interaction, I'm sure you already understand that.

Maybe they have a problem. Maybe they want to sell you something. Maybe they want to thank you and provide a testimonial for something. These little contacts can lead to bigger and better things, but don't count on it - a lot of the time someone just asks you for a bunch of information that if you explained to them, you could write a book!

You don't have to respond to people who contact you, but I would recommend at least looking at every message. You never know when you can use it to your benefit. You could put "kind words from subscribers" on a testimonial page, you could partner with someone on a product, you could meet people that want to promote YOU and your blog. You'll never know unless you allow people to contact you.

So what's better, just providing an email address, or providing a contact form?

Many have stated that they get a lot of spam with contact forms. However, these days you can find a good contact form plugin, or service, or code, or add-on in a theme or blogging service that has anti-spam captchas. So I would say as long as you are protecting yourself from spam, then a contact form is perfect.

I also like contact forms because then people don't have to copy and paste your email address into a new tab where their email is, create a subject line, then add their message, then send. Instead, they are able to just insert in their name, email, and message right on your blog, and hit "send".

However, some people abuse contact forms for that very reason. You won't deal with automated spam, but you may come across some self-created spam. Some may take advantage of your contact form and leave you 500 messages that say "haha". That means 500 emails that you have to go through with the same stupid message.

So the next best thing is to just include your email address on your blog - either on a contact page, or your about page, or both.

However, again this can lead to spam - let me explain... If you simply put your email address as-is (email@email.com), some automated spammers may pick up your email, automatically add it to a list, and automatically be sent messages in the future. It sucks, so don't let this happen to you.

Instead, break up your email a little like this: email [at] email [dot] com

This way, it doesn't show up as an email address to automated spammers and scammers. And, it's easy enough for everyone to understand that [at] means "@" and [dot] means ".".

19

Powerful, Engaging Images

Don't tell me you haven't noticed the influx in huge images on blogs, facebook pages, profiles, twitter, and other places online?

More people are responding to images rather than text, and of course you know the reason why: It's because our attention spans are getting smaller.

Okay, enough jokes about the human race, but I'm totally serious. If you have a blog with no images, you are pretty much dead in the water. If you have a blog with images that aren't powerful and engaging, then you are only halfway there.

People are seeing more images than ever online today, mainly because they don't have the will to read a few paragraphs unless they are able to view something engaging in the process.

A simple full-column image will do the trick.

When I say full-column, I mean if your content area of your blog is 700px wide, then your image should be 700px wide (and your own desired height).

This will work on most blogs, but of course if you like to change your images from time to time, that's fine.

You want your image to present a positive image, or maybe controversial, or maybe funny or shocking - but whatever type of image you show, an easy way to get more interaction is to add text to your image.

You don't have to do this for all your images, but the more the better. When you add text, you are allowing your visitors to both be engaged by an image as well as reading your desired text at the same time.

So what text do you put on the image?

It will be different for every blog. If you are all about success/entrepreneur/online biz, then maybe add an inspiring quote or a quick business tip. If you are a comical blog, add something that will make your audience laugh.

Just be sure that you are including images in your blog posts at all times. It's not a picture perfect science that you'll get more visitors or more leads, but you'll definitely engage at least a handful of your visitors more than they would have been, which is always a good thing.

20

Easy To Read Text (Bigger Is Better)

I hope you're finding the book helpful so far. This first handful of chapters includes lots of basics, but I know there are a lot of you who are finding the nice little tips within tips.

Have you really browsed around and looked at the text on various blogs? Some of it is not pretty.

First and foremost, don't use color-on-color text. I'm talking about the blue text with the orange background, or the green text on a pink background. Save that for myspace, let your blog be simple.

You want people being able to read your blog posts easily, and consume your content with ease.

Black text on a white background works best among all blogs. I would suggest holding off on the black backgrounds, as it makes people's eyes tired. If you want to go for white text, go with a dark shade of gray as the background. And if you are going to use any sort of color on the background, start with gray and then tint it slightly to the color you want to use. You don't want a bright solid color, but you might want to give a cool blue essence, or a hot orange flare.

This next tip is not extremely important, but I find that it helps a lot, so I'm including it.

The tip is bigger is better. Don't use 12 point font on your blog - some people won't be able to read it! At least increase the size of your text a little bit.

But honestly, I would increase the size of your text a lot. You'll find that some browsers display text differently, as well as different devices. If you have bigger text, you are allowing more people to read your posts with ease.

The only reason I say this tip isn't extremly important is because of the increase in devices being able to resize text. In almost every browser, I'm able to change the size of the font, or at least the size of the entire web page to make reading easier. Even web pages I read on my Kindle Fire have the option to make the text and web pages bigger or smaller.

But for the people who don't go that extra mile to read your blog, you can make it easier on them by increasing the size of your text.

Of course you probably already thought of this, but increasing the size of your text means instantly longer posts (in a sense of webpage height). People will be scrolling down further to read the entire post, and will pass by all of the great things you have in your sidebar.

21

Creative Design And Theme

Back in the day, if you wanted color and borders and backgrounds and sidebars and footers and headers and columns, and all the other design elements that allows your blog to be shown, you would have to code up a CSS stylesheet in order to do it. Even further back in the day, it all had to be done in one document!

But now, we have these great things called themes.

If you want your blog to be successful, you need a good theme. Some themes are free, some themes cost a few dollars, some cost hundreds and thousands. Some have little functionality and design features, while some give you everything you need and then some.

Every blog is different - different content, different niches, different writers, different owners. If you want your blog to be unique, you must have a unique theme.

When looking for a theme, make sure you take note of all of the features of each one. Some themes have SEO features, some have extreme design features. You want a theme that will enable you to click a few buttons and have your site colors changed. Then a few more clicks, and your text is different. A dozen clicks later, and you have a full working sidebar.

Besides functionality, you want your theme's and blog's design to stand out. And above all, you want it to look professional, even if your site is about fart jokes. There is a difference between a badly designed fart joke site and a professionally designed fart joke site.

If your blog doesn't look the way you want, CHANGE YOUR THEME. Even if your blog is 10 years old, it's okay to go through a theme change. If you don't change, you could be left behind.

22

Easy And Clear Navigation

Clear navigation comes with a good theme. Get a good theme, and you'll be able to have a lot of navigation choices.

Navigation in a sense is just how people get around your blog. It can be categories, tags, inter-site links, but is most commonly referred to as the navigation bar.

The navigation bar is usually displayed above or below your header, but is always toward the top of the blog. It is also shown on all pages (unless you have a splash page or sales page where you wouldn't include it). Common pages included in your navigation bar include home page, about page, contact page, blog, products, free gift - sometimes people include their main categories in their navigation bar.

What you include in your navigation bar is up to you. Just ask yourself one question - "When someone falls on my site, how do they navigate around, what pages can they access, if they visited each page in the navigation bar in order, what would that be like?

I know your blog visitors aren't stupid, but sometimes you just need to give them a little direction in order to get them to go to the places you want on your blog.

Since most people put their about page right after their home page, people tend to click on that navigation button or link to go to the about page (which is why I explained earlier why you need a SELLING about page).

If you have a free book you want them to download, make a separate page on your blog, add the page to your navigation bar as a link or button, and you'll find more people getting to that page.

If you want to add your categories to your navigation, my recommendation is to NOT mix your categories with your pages. Some blogs have a top navigation for pages, and a navigation below the header for the categories. If you must have categories, splitting these up makes it easier for your visitors to understand what it is they are looking at.

23

Don't Go On Plugin Overload!

I know some of you are smiling right now. Is your blog on plugin overload?

I would usually say "it's okay if it is", but it's really not okay. Do you know how many people you are losing because of a slow-loading site (which is caused by way too many active plugins)?

Go ahead and use the various services out there that tell you how fast your site loads. I know Alexa keeps those stats public, and there are dozens of other sites and services that do about the same thing.

And it's not so much the quantity of plugins as it is the amount of bandwith each one uses on your server. Some social plugins tend to make sites load a tad bit slower. Then, when you combine multiple sharing and social plugins with email plugins, and ad plugins, and all the other plugins you have on your blog, your site will run a lot slower than it should.

Besides slow loading blogs, too many plugins (especially ones that show up physically on your blog [as opposed to background plug-ins]) can make your site look extremely cluttered and unprofessional.

And as I'll say again in this book, you really need a clear CTA (call to action) on your blog, on every single page really. And having 20 different plugins and widgets and social code on your blog doesn't give your visitors a clear sense of what you want them to do.

So, only use the plugins you really need on your blog. And if your blog is running slow, find out which plugin(s) is making your site slow, and find a replacement! There are alternatives for EVERYTHING these days.

24

"Bookmark This Site" Button

Everyone knows about bookmarking, but do you use it effectively to generate repeat visitors to your blog?

I mean come on people - this is one of those tasks that takes less than 60 seconds, and will 100% make your blog more successful. In other words, it couldn't hurt your site, and will only help it.

Put it this way: Sometimes people aren't logged in to twitter and facebook, and don't want to log in to follow or like you. Sometimes people don't want to give their email address (or don't have one!) to get email updates from you. Some people don't know what an RSS feed is. But who's to say that these people aren't interested in your blog? Sure, they don't trust you enough to give you their email address or credit card info for a payment, but they might like a way to just save your blog so they can easily come back sometime in the future.

Of course it's better to have these people subscribe via email, or have them get updated publications in an RSS feed, but for those who just won't do those things, you should always give them the chance to bookmark your site. Bookmarking is great because it works in any browser, and on any computer (for the most part, of course there are always a couple odd exceptions).

There are many ways to do this, I know of 3 somewhat well:

1. Code up your own bookmark link. Or pay someone $5 to do it. Of course, many of us aren't that tech-savvy, so only code your own if you know what you are doing. The last thing you want is some error on your blog that makes it not work at all.
2. Use/Buy a bookmarking link plugin. You can find one for free, or buy one to use on your blog.

3. Some themes come with bookmarking features built in. Again, all it takes is a little research, and you'll find some great themes, plugins, and services that come with these features.

Don't pass up on this tip. It only takes a minute or two to get this up on your blog, and you'll see at least a little bit of an increase in repeat visitors over the next few months. You see, some of these tips and strategies are simple to do and easy to implement, while others are more advanced and take more time to implement. I'm going to continue with a lot of the little things you can do to make your blog more successful, and then we'll get deeper into the world of professional blogging.

25

"Tweet This Quote/Line/Tip" Content Links

This has become more popular over time, and I believe it to be a nice addition to any blog.

Call it what you want, "Tweet This content links", "Click To Tweet links", "Tweet links", it will definitely add a lot of interaction on your website.

You probably have some sort of link or button to allow people to follow you. You probably have a social twitter tweet link for each one of your articles and pieces of blog content. Now add in these "tweet links" inside your post, and you've got the TWITTER TRIFECTA!

You might have seen these twitter links used on some popular blogs before. Basically, the idea is - Your visitor scrolls down the page reading your article. They get to a point where there is an inspirational quote, or funny line, or a highlighted point. Then, there is a link saying "click here to tweet this [insert the blank]".

If you have a long post, you can have 3 or 4 of these tweet links, and get even more interaction!

The reason more people use these "tweet this one line/quote" links as opposed to your "tweet this entire post" link is because instead of tweeting a blatant link to an article to their followers, they tweet the line/quote/saying/tip to their followers, which gives these tweets the chance of being shared further.

Of course, when you include these tweet links, you'll want to include the link (shortened) to the post the line is included in, so when people tweet your quote/line, they will also be sending out a link to your blog post.

So, how do you do this?

Well, there's obviously a way to code this, as is anything really. Right now, people are using this code:

http://twitter.com/home/?status=YOURSTATUSHERE

But of course, that could change any minute, and you don't get the same styling features as your second option - a tweet link service.

Right now, the site and service that makes these tweet links for you is called "Click To Tweet". But again, this will change, so I suggest searching around for an easy option - one you can set up with ease and use on every new post you publish.

Don't overdo it with these tweet links - however, I like to think the more the merrier. I mean heck, it's part of your content anyway, and the only thing you are adding is a tiny link that says "Click to tweet".

26

Show Off Your Big Numbers

There's no shame in being popular, and one way you can influence your blog visitors is to show off your big numbers.

Do you have a lot of twitter followers? How about facebook fans/likes? Testimonials or people you'ved helped? Comments?

Even if it's your visitors or pageviews that are high, you should start showing these numbers off to your blog!

If you were to just have your normal blog, and hide or don't show your big numbers, your visitors would have to click a few times, and possibly leave your site before they see what type of a following you have.

But, if you were to show off your big numbers, the people who want to know what type of following you have will be able to see just how many people you influence.

If you have 5 twitter followers, 34 facebook likes, and 13 email subscribers, DON'T SHOW THOSE NUMBERS OFF! Increase your following, or show different numbers. You might only have 5 twitter followers, but maybe you've gotten 500 comments total on your blog that you want to show off.

The point is, people respond to big numbers. If 10,000 people are following you, of course people are going to see that number when you show it. And most of them will take a minute to think, "If this blog has this many followers, maybe I should listen to what they have to say".

I'm not saying to go get fake followers or fake likes, or comment on a bunch of your posts. Use the other tips and strategies in this book to your advantage, then show off the big numbers to your visitors to really put the icing on the cake.

Big numbers basically tells people, "Everyone else is here, why aren't you?"

27

GETTING RID OF BLOG SPAM

Any blogger who's anyone gets blog spam. It happens, and there are ways of getting rid of it.

First we have email spam, and as I explained before in the "contact/about page" chapters, you should avoid displaying your full email address on your website, and you should only use a contact form if you have anti-spam captchas in place.

Next, we have the even more common type of spam: comment spam.

Some people could care less about what you or your blog has to say, and are only looking to benefit themselves. So, they go on your blog, and post 100 comments on all your articles saying "click here to visit my site".

Maybe it's their own site, maybe it's an affiliate promotion - Somehow, they get paid to do it, or they wouldn't do it in the first place.

The first thing I would suggest is using Akismet anti-spam plugin on your blog. I'm pretty sure you can use that plugin on any blog for free, and all you have to do is get a validation code from the Akismet plugin to start using it.

What these types of anti-spam plugins do is reference your incoming blog comments to common types of spam, including referencing spam already posted on other blogs as well as not publishing comments with a certain amount of links. You can also program your plugin so that it doesn't post comments with URLs, or so that it doesn't post comments with certain keywords or websites.

Besides anti-spam plugins, you should regularly (at least once a week) take a brief look at the "comments" area in your blog dashboard. You don't have to go through each post, all your comments are in the same place in your dashboard.

Just scroll through all of the comments, and check to see if there are any you want to get rid of.

Even if you get 100 comments a day, meaning 700 per week, and checked your comments once a week, it will still only take you a few minutes to scroll through your comments. You don't have to read each one word for word, just make sure no one is spamming your comment sections.

Spam is bad, and makes you and your blog look bad as well.

Do what you can to get rid of it, and use anti-spam plugins to get rid of the junk automatically.

28

Gravatar / Site Comment Thumbnails

This isn't some huge strategy to get you lots of traffic or anything like that, but can prove to be a valuable asset to your blog.

What I'm talking about is your blog comment thumbnails - those little pictures/thumbnails/images that show up next to each person who comments on your blog.

Sure you want people commenting, but what happens when they all show up as the same thumbnail? You know that little "mystery man" image?

When you don't have any thumbnails or avatars in place, everyone who comments on your blog looks like the same person (besides the different names).

Of course, people will understand that they are different people, but at first glance, it looks like a robot pumped out a bunch of text and threw it up on your blog.

In WordPress, you can choose different types of avatar groups to use as your comment thumbnails. There's a robot group, a gravatar group, little monsters, and tons of other types of avatar groups.

When you choose one, all of the comments on your blog will immediately have their own unique image thumbnails next to them.

Again, this isn't a huge make-or-break strategy, but it definitely adds a sense of real communication and interaction on your blog, and that's the most important aspect you want to show off.

29

SPICE UP YOUR HEADLINES!

Have you been caught up in this before? You write a bunch of AMAZING content, but then no one clicks over to your article you just spent hours writing?

Well, it could be because your headline wasn't interesting enough.

You've heard this strategy before, but are you using it to it's full potential?

When your blog post is published, it will be shared. It will be shared among facebook, among twitter, among linkedin and digg and stumbleupon and 50 other websites.

But when it is shared, do other people become interested and click over to your blog?

You see, it's not enough to share the content. You need the people you're sharing the content with to share it even further, and so on. An easy way to do that is spicing up your headlines.

There are lots of different ways of spicing up your headlines.

Use these types of words: easy, shocking, discover, secrets, tips, strategies, free, simple, more, increase.

These words are what some call power words. Really, it's just a psychological thing. People respond to power words.

But really, people just want things easy, they want to be entertained, they want to solve a problem.

Your headline is the very first thing people see, both on your blog, and when the specific post is being shared. Focus on the headline above all, as this is what's going to first attract people to your blog.

Once they are there, it's up to you to follow the other strategies to have a successful blog, but this step will get more people over there.

30

SOME BLOGS HAVE GREAT FORUMS

Before I get into forum creation, let me just tell you one thing: Forums don't work for everyone. In fact, they take a lot more time to manage and make successful than a blog.

Now, although forums don't work for all blogs, there are a good handful of instances in which a forum would make a great addition to a blog.

Why were forums first built? To allow people to communicate with eachother. So technically, if you want people communicating more with eachother ON YOUR BLOG, then you should create a forum.

The setup is the easy part (sort of), it's the time it takes to manage, administrate, and keep up with your forum that is more time consuming.

Most hosting packages include the scripts and features to set up your own forum, and it is usually some sort of point and click interface, which means no difficult coding on your end.

Right now, pretty much everyone I know that has a forum uses the free script phpBB. This is also what my hosting company uses in their hosting package.

Choose where you want your forum (I suggest something like forum.YourBlog.com), and if you don't know how, ask your hosting company (HostGator has 24/7 live support).

Then, choose what discussion areas and topics you want. Finally, publish your forum, and start promoting it to get people talking!

Now, I don't want to make it seem like starting a forum is the best idea for your blog, or easy for that matter. It does take a lot of work to manage, especially when you start getting people posting in your forum at all hours of the day and night.

But, if you want more interaction on your blog, a forum is a nice route to go.

31

Make Your Blog Mobile-Friendly

Ask any millionaire who currently makes their money online-only (who is planning for the future), and they will tell you that mobile is the future.

And not just phones, but any device that isn't a computer.

Today we have smart phones, androids, iphones, ipads, kindles, nooks, and dozens of other popular mobile devices, and tomorrow there will be brand new mobile devices!

The point is, EVERYONE is going to have some sort of mobile device one day. Is your site optimized for mobile devices?

If you don't know how, let me tell you again - it's easy.

Sometimes a blog theme package will come with the feature of being able to mobilize your site. If so, use it! Go through the few steps it takes to get a mobile version of your site published. It will only take a couple minutes.

Sometimes the hosting company you are signed up with will have a feature for making your site mobile-friendly.

And sometimes, you will just have to use some other company or service to make your mobile blog.

By making your site available on mobile, you are first making your site load much faster. Most webpages aren't optimized for mobile, and can take minutes to load. Even if it only takes 10 seconds, that's still longer than some people want. With a mobile site, your blog will load on people's mobile devices in seconds.

Besides a faster loading mobile blog, you also have the extreme benefit of being one of those blogs that is available on mobile devices. People will start to save your site on their phones and other devices, people will come back in the future - some will even get an email from you on their phone, click on a link to your blog, and be reading your content on your mobile site immediately.

Trust me, mobile is the future, be there.

32

Have LOTS Of Posts

There's actually been a lot of talk about how many posts a blog should have, as well as the increase and decrease of visitors a blog will receive depending on the number of posts they have.

The conclusion was: MORE posts is BETTER.

I'm not saying you should go add 1,000 posts to your blog tonight, I'm just saying that you should be thinking about how often you post to your blog. Most bloggers don't blog enough.

It will take time to build up to a lot of posts and content on your blog, but it's possible, and very beneficial to your success.

The studies that were done basically concluded that a blog with hundreds of posts will receive more interaction and more visitors than a blog with only 5 posts.

You might be thinking that was expected, but a lot of people use to argue saying that more posts doesn't mean more visitors. However, I think they were just a little emotional and pissed off at the auto-bloggers who used to be able to pump out 1,000 articles in minutes to a blog.

When you have 100 or more posts on your blog, it allows people to move around and really explore your blog. More pageviews, more visitors, more chance at comments, interaction, sharing - it just helps.

So don't go post a bunch of articles tonight thinking your blog will change overnight - But, start to post more, and really build up a large quantity of blog posts, all while continuing to add lots of value.

33

Short Posts VS Long Posts

So you know you need lots of posts on your blog to get more interaction, but what about the length?

I'm sure you've seen some blogs with lots of tiny 100 word-or-less posts, while other blogs only have multi-page, 1,000+ word articles. So who's right and wrong?

The answer is: BOTH!

Don't you hate that answer, "both"? But, it's true, the length of your posts don't matter much, as long as you diversify.

If you have 1,000 posts that are 10 words each, you won't get much traction. If you have 10 posts that are 10,000 words each, you may get more traction, but still not the type you are looking for.

But, if you have a lot of tiny posts, a lot of medium posts, a few long posts, and really just a variety of lengths, it helps out much more. Some people like reading for awhile, some people like getting all the info quick. You can make both of these people happy.

Another very important reason you want to diversify the length of your posts is because you never know what kinds of algorithm changes the search engines are going to make. If one day they decide to penalize a blog that only has short posts or only has long posts, you will be less likely to be heavily slapped or removed from search engines.

34

Micro Blog Posts (Blog Tweets)

As I've said before, the attention spans of the human race are getting shorter.

Sometimes, people don't want to read a 1,000 word article. Heck, sometimes they don't even want to read a 200 word article. Sometimes, all someone needs is a nice, short, to-the-point micro post that they can read in less than a minute and be more than satisfied with.

Unless you are really lazy, I wouldn't make micro posts exclusive to your blog - I would mix in some short/medium length and long posts in with these micro posts.

A micro post is really just a small blog post that can be said in a few sentences. You can even do one-sentence blog posts.

Search engines might not pick it up as easily at first because there isn't a lot of content within the post, but if your one sentence post is powerful enough to generate some sharing and some media buzz, then search engines may very well start to pick up on your micro posts.

But it's not all about the search engines, and you should never rely solely on search engines.

These posts should be quick, to-the-point, but should also provide some sort of value. Maybe you share a quote, maybe you ask a question, maybe you give a quick tip.

I also call these "blog tweets" because they are usually short enough to be tweeted. You can share your entire blog post in a tweet, add the link to the post on your blog, and you could get double the sharing - from your blog AND twitter.

If your posts are longer than tweet-length, you can alway summarize your post, or just write as much as you can, and at the end, put 3 dots (...).

The key with these micro posts is to give 1 tiny piece of value to the person who reads it. If you want it to be funny, your visitor should laugh. If you want it to be serious, your visitor should be taking a minute or two to think. If you want it to be inspiring, your visitor should be motivated and inspired after reading it.

If you can package little pieces of value into micro posts, you'll find a lot more interaction on your blog. Your visitor won't feel like they would be wasting time to comment after reading an article for 5 or 10 minutes, because they just read your entire post in 5 seconds. You'll get plenty of shares, likes, and comments.

35

USE GOOD TRACKING AND ANALYTICS

No blog should be without good tracking and analytics.

Luckily, because of the availability of great free services, you are able to get the most professional tracking for free. There are many ways to track your site, and you can track anything from visitors to IP addresses to logins to what countries people are from, even the keywords people are searching for to get to your site.

All of these stats can tell you a lot about your blog, and really help lead you down the right path. They also tell you when things are going horribly wrong, and allow you to catch the little issues before they become huge problems.

Most use Google Analytics. I recommend it as well. If you don't want to bother with installing analytics code or signing up for services, you should at a minimum be checking up on the stats your hosting company gives you.

These stats tell you a lot. Check out the incoming search terms. These are terms that people are searching for on search engines, and then finding your blog. You can analyze what questions or keywords they are typing in to figure out what post they probably landed on. And if someone is searching for something that you don't have on your site, but they get to your site anyway, maybe it's time you posted some content about that topic.

You can also see your most popular and most visited pages, which gives you the opportunity of showing off these posts more, and really get the blog juice flowing.

It's also nice to see where you are getting traffic from, how long people stay on your site, what days of the week are most popular for your blog, as well as the daily pageviews. You will notice drops and spikes, and can probably attribute them to a certain promotion you did or a new batch of blog posts you published.

No matter what type of blog you run, you need to check on your stats from time to time. Don't check your stats multiple times daily. I would suggest either picking a time once a day if you are impatient (or right when you wake up, then right before you sleep), or just check on it every week or so. It all depends on how often you blog, and really how serious you are about blogging. If you are serious, and want your blog to be a success and make you some good money, then stats and analytics are a must.

36

PERMALINK STRUCTURE (BEST SEO PRACTICES)

Most blog systems and content management systems (like WordPress) use what are called permalinks.

Basically, permalinks are the URLs that your blogging system assigns to your new posts you add to your blog.

In WordPress, there are a few options you can choose. And of course, I would recommend choosing your desired permalink structure at the very beginning of your blog; But, better late than never.

Under settings, then permalink settings, there are 4 options as of right now in my dashboard:

Default: http://myblog.com/?p=123

Day and name: http://myblog.com/2015/05/10/post-name/

Month and name: http://myblog.com/2015/05/post-name/

Numeric: http://myblog.com/archives/123

There is also a 5th option, "custom structure", which allows you to choose any custom URL string you want.

I would suggest choosing one that includes your post name. The 'day and name' and 'month and name' choices are good. But creating your own custom structure is better for SEO. If you want your blog posts to be picked up in the search engines a little bit easier, just go with /%postname%/ , and your blog will display your post URLs like this: http://myblog.com/post-name

But, if you want to choose one of WordPress's (or another blog platform's) choices, then go with the dates that include your post name. This is also a good choice, because people reading your blog post can look at the URL and find out when it was published. But of course, if most of your posts include outdated information, and the dates show it, then don't count on those blog posts being shared forever.

37

Know Basic HTML

You don't have to be a genius to know HTML. Heck, my 5 year old nephew knows basic html coding!

You don't even need to know how to code an entire page with HTML code. As long as you know the basics, you'll be fine.

The most common HTML codes you will use on your blog include:

- hyperlinks
- download links
- images
- formatting like center/left/right align
- line/page breaks
- paragraph
- bold/italicize/underline

And of course the list goes on and on - but those are the ones you NEED to know in order to publish some good looking content.

Honestly, do you want to know where I learned ALL of my HTML skills from? - www.w3schools.com

That site basically gives you every HTML, CSS, Javascript, and others like ASP .NET, XML, web services, PHP, SQL, and more. But for your blog, all you need to know is HTML - which right now is the very first tab on the w3schools site.

This site and many others make it easy for the coding newbie. Seriously, there's not much you need to learn about coding for simple stuff on your blog. You can honestly learn everything I listed above within a few minutes, and after typing the codes over and over for a few days, it'll start to get EASY. You'll be flying through code, and your friends and family will wonder how in the world you learned this mystical coding language!

But really, you don't want your blog to be a huge sea of text. And you don't want to rely 100% on the point and click features of inserting images and video and other media and text into your posts. By learning some basic HTML, you are giving yourself the advantage of always being able to use simple code for any type of web page building or publishing you do online.

38

LEARN SEO AND KEYWORDS

SEO = Search Engine Optimization, and you need to know how it works.

SEO is sort of like HTML in a sense that you don't NEED to use it in order to be succesful, but it will definitely help out with anything you do online, not just blogging.

Search engine optimization is exactly as it sounds - optimizing your website/blog for search engines. It is the act in which you make your blog more popular in order for search engines to pick up on your blog more, list it more frequently in their algorithm, list it for more keywords, list it higher in the ranking.

And it's not just making your blog more popular, it's getting search engines to notice you. Then, when they notice you, how popular you really are will match up against how popular other websites are.

I would be a fool to tell you that there are only a few things you need to do in order to get SEO'd. Search engine algorithms change all the time, and there will never be a clear set of guaranteed-to-work SEO tasks.

However, there are 2 things in particular that will never die - keywords and backlinks.

No matter what, search engines will HAVE TO analyze the keywords both on your site AND pointing to your site (in a backlink). If they stopped analyzing keywords, they would only be able to rank sites and pages based on popularity, and people wouldn't be able to search using keywords anymore, because they would never find anything they were looking for!

Also, backlinks will never die because they are the easiest way to determine the general popularity of a website or blog (or specific page). But it's not just about the quantity of backlinks, they need to be from high-page-rank sources.

Use the Google Keyword Tool to analyze popular keywords you can use for your blog posts. Then USE THEM. After that, go out and get some backlinks to your blog post or blog in general.

These things, as well as hundreds of other tiny factors, are what makes SEO work for you. Use them to your advantage, keep building your links consistently over time, and keep writing valuable content with researched keywords, add a little social media, and the search engines will love you.

39

Link Personal Blog To Business Blog

All of these tips and strategies can be used for both personal and business blogs. But whatever you are using these for, it's always important to link up your personal blog to your business blog.

For the sake of not having 2 completely opposite chapters, I'm going to assume the blog you are trying to make successful is NOT a personal blog - meaning you don't post updates about your life only.

I've only seen a few people link their blogs together successfully, and it seems to work a great deal for them. It's not like every time someone visits one blog, they hop on over to the other. But, there is definitely a greater sense of "I'm a human, here to help!".

Many who browse through a 'business' blog (blog you make money from/for business/branded/etc.) will check out the blog posts, but even when they enjoy the content, it still doesn't give them a true personal touch. Some people want that personal touch, sometimes. That's why you have 2 blogs (or more). One for business/money, one for personal. Don't combine the two.

When you link your personal blog to your main blog, you are able to connect with your readers and visitors in a more personal way. It's like having a HUGE about me page, except instead of having one page with limited space, you are free to post on your entire personal blog.

Your visitors will really get to know you this way, which in most cases is a great thing! They can see who you are, see what you are up to, find out what other projects, blogs, websites, and stuff you are working on.

And of course if you don't have a personal blog yet, GET ONE. YourName.com, YourNickName.com, VariationOfYourName.com - do it.

40

SELL AD SPACE (ADS IN GENERAL)

When your blog becomes more popular, and gets more traffic and interaction, you will start to get noticed by companies and individuals that would like to advertise on your blog.

You can solve these people's needs by selling ad space on your blog. There are so many different ways of doing this, and it is one of the most common forms of blogs monetization.

Most people start with Google Adsense, or some type of CPC advertising (cost per click). This is the easiest to setup, and the easiest to get banned from. Every old blogger I know has gotten their Adsense account disabled. Most people have the thought that their accounts could be shut down at any moment, and you should have the same thought if you decide to go with one of these companies.

You also have CPM ads, or Cost Per Thousand (M) Impressions - meaning you get paid not when someone clicks, but a set amount every time 1,000 people view an ad on your site. These are easy to set up as well, but you won't make any type of solid income unless your blog gets millions of page views each day (which I'm guessing is not the case, YET).

I've seen a lot of blogs going with flat rate pricing, which is set to monthly display ads and monthly pricing (or any pricing scheme you want). You can go with something like OIOPublisher, and pay a one time fee for their plugin, and keep 100% commission on the ads you sell - Or, you could use something like BuySellAds.com, where you don't pay anything (join free), and then they take a percentage of each ad sale you make.

Whatever you decide is the best form of ad monetization on your site will of course work. With flat rate ads, you actually have to make an ad sale before you get money.

With CPC and CPM, all you need are the views and the clicks (both types will never give you instant commissions - usually at least 1 month after the last day of the month).

You won't make a million dollars from ads alone. Only a few have done it - it's less likely than winning the Olympics. Selling ad space on your blog is fine, but you should also be thinking about other forms of monetization as well, not just the easy kinds.

41

Focus On The Human Before The Robot

I know you've heard this before, but now it's time to grind it in deep into your brain.

You can do all the SEO, plugins, hacks, shortcuts and workarounds that you want, it's still not going to mean anything close to what your human visitors mean to your blog.

When Google dies tomorrow, will your blog survive?

Think about that. What if Google disappeared? What if all the search engines disappeared? Would you be screwed?

Nothing is more important than your human visitors. Don't spend ALL your time on SEO and links and technical stuff. Spend more time figuring out how you can help solve people's problems, entertain people, make people laugh, teach someone something, make them more successful, more inspired, more motivated.

If you focus on the human before the robot, the robots will take notice. But only spend time on robots, and never on humans, and you'll never have a big following of people craving your blog content.

But back to search engines being shut down. It will never happen. But what if Google drops you, slaps you, puts you in the sandbox? You need to have the connections beyond the people coming in from search engines. Same with social networks. What happens when your account gets disabled or shut down? Do your "fans" and "followers" even know who you are? If you told them your account got shut down, and they need to re-follow you, would they?

That's why an email list is super-important. When everything else crumbles, you will still be able to send an email out to all of your subscribers telling them what to do next.

Just remember that like there is a person writing your blog posts (you), there is also a person reading your blog posts (your visitor).

42

People LOVE Free Gifts

The title of this chapter says it all, people love free gifts.

It's like opening a present on your birthday, getting something that you didn't pay for, and although you know what the present could be, you're still not sure exactly what's inside.

This works the same way on blogs, and really anywhere, online and offline.

We touched a little on free gifts in previous chapters, but I wanted to dedicate an entire chapter to free gifts because of how important I think they are to the success of your blog.

I'm not talking about buying all your visitors iPads and Kindles or anything, I'm talking about DIGITAL gifts (and not the lame facebook ones either!).

It could be a 30 minute audio, a special 'secret' video, an e-book (PDF), and all sorts of other types of digital content.

Many people who visit blogs are getting tired of just reading post after post. They want something different! So, to give them what they want, you can give them the same value as your blog posts, but just package the content differently.

If your blog post "All About Caring For Your Iguana" is extremely popular, you can expand on the information included in that blog post, and give extra tips on taking care of an iguana. Maybe it could be an audio track of the exact steps needed to feed your iguana. It could also be a video showing off iguana tricks.

You can choose to either give away your gift publicly, in which you would post a download link directly on your blog, or you can make the content private so that they must join your email list in order to get the gift. As you can see, a digital gift can not only give you some great traffic, but can also get you email subscribers who you can email other stuff to in the future.

Just make sure your free gift has more content and value than a blog post, but less content than you would put in a complete product. Keep it short, make it valuable, and make sure you plug your blog within the content of the free gift to ensure people know where it came from, and where to go to get more info.

43

Solve People's Problems With Your Content

This goes hand in hand with caring about the human more than the robot.

When you create content and publish it on your blog, you want to publish that content with the intention of solving someone's problem, making someone's day, further accelerating someone's skill or greatness.

You want people to love you when they're done reading your content, and nothing works better than the content itself - solve someone's problem, and they'll love you forever. You're a blogger, and if you've been a blogger long enough, you've heard the coined term content is king. I believe in that 100%, it's the keywords that get people to your website or blog, but it's the content you create that will get people to come back again.

It's not hard to solve someone's problem.

Think of the problems you used to come across when blogging. If you have been using WordPress for awhile, do you remember the first time you ever looked at the interface? I didn't know what did what. But now, I'm able to work my around dozens of blogs, and I know where everything is and what everything does. There will always be people that don't know as much as you do about a certain topic or subject. That right there is your core audience, because you can actually help them.

You can find out what people's problems are in your niche by searching around other blogs, forums, ask/answer sites - you can look in the comment sections of pretty much ANY web page, and find someone having a related problem that they still can't solve.

When you know the common problems in your niche, you just have to solve them yourself, and then show other people how to solve it - OR just interview or accept a guest post of someone who knows more than you and your audience.

People love helpful blogs. It allows them to learn about many different subjects, topics, tips/strategies, and also can get your blog posts a lot more comments. People don't write comments on lazy robot posts. People write comments on posts that truly overdeliver.

44

Allow Comment-Linking

First of all, you should obviously already have some sort of comment system or plugin installed on your blog.

But you shouldn't stop there. Besides simply allowing comments, you should also allow your commenters to link their name to their website.

If you are already doing this, good for you, I'm sure you don't have huge issues with getting comments.

Other bloggers, competitors, and really anyone who has a URL to a page of their's love to write comments on blogs that llow them to link to their website, or blog, or sales page, or facebook page, or twitter, etc.

This is different from "allowing URLs in comments".

This has to do with the name of the person leaving the comment. On some blogs, you would write your name, "John Clark", your email, and your comment. If your blog has the "website" field enabled in the comment section, then people would write their name, "John Clark", their email, their comment, AND their website, "http://JohnsReallyCoolAwesomeBlog.com". Then, their name would be the link to the website when their comment appears.

It's important that you allow your visitors and commenters to link to their website or blog via comments - it gets more people to comment, because besides making a connection, these commenters are also being allowed to promote themselves in a good way.

You'll also find that if you have "comment-luv" comments or "do-follow" comment links, you'll get a huge burst of interaction, because now not only are people able to comment and promote themselves, but the link they post will also be picked up in the search engines and will add to their own rank and popularity.

Just make sure you're at least letting people link their names (website/URL field in comments) in your comment section, and you will start to get more comments and sharing on your blog.

45

The Poll Advantage

Yes, POLLS. Polls are one of the biggest hidden advantages a blogger could ever ask for.

People do polls. It's quick , it's easy, and you get to see results in the click of a button to see how you match up against other people who are answering the same poll question. Polls are addicting.

This is one of those tips that I would hear someone talk about, then dismiss it and say "yeah, I see it works, but I'll get to it later".

Don't be one of those people. In fact, put a poll on your blog right now! It will only take 5 minutes, and you'll have a brand new piece of content on your blog that people can take action with. You may even get some comments about the poll.

There are dozens of free poll code websites that let you choose the questions, the style and dimensions of the poll box, and then they shoot out a code that you put on your website (or in this case, a blog post).

And if you don't want to use one of these website services, just search "polls" in the WordPress plugin directory, and again you'll have dozens of choices.

It's best if you ask a question that people can answer in seconds. Like... "How much money do you want to make per month?" Then you have a. $1,000 b. $5,000 c. $10,000 d. $25,000+

Also, make sure the question directly relates to your niche. Don't ask a question just for the sake of asking it. In fact, after you get a nice handful of answers, you can post a followup to the poll in which you explain what people answered, and then maybe give some insight or extra info that these people could benefit from.

It's easier to start a conversation by having someone click one button than it is to get them to email you, call you, even comment on your blog. A poll makes it easy for the lazy people to contribute, too.

46

Keeping Your Writing Consistent

I shouldn't need to tell you this, but because I've seen inconsistent writing on so many blogs, I figured this needed to be mentioned.

Your blog shouldn't look like it was written by 10 different authors. Everything should flow, especially the style of writing.

Most of the time, when someone begins to enjoy a blog, they expect to continue to enjoy it. But if your blog contains inconsistencies, and your writing starts to become different, your posts get laid out in a different way, your text is larger or smaller - you will make some of these people mad.

And even if you don't make them mad, you're still giving them a reason to leave your blog. "Well, it was good while it lasted" and "There was a few good pieces in there" just doesn't cut it anymore. You want people reading your blog and viewing your content as much as they possibly can, and it all starts with a consistent writing style.

Haven't you ever been to a blog that you just can't wait to read the next post? That's how you need to position your blog. Make it so that when someone finishes one post, they can't wait to get to the next one, and the next one, and the next one.

And on the contrary, if your blog isn't doing as well as you'd like, and your posts aren't as consistent as you'd like them to be, change your writing style.

Go ahead, change up your style a little here and a little there, and see how your visitors react. When you start to get more interaction, more visitors, and more people commenting about your posts, you know you are on the right track.

47

PASSION + DESIRE = SUCCESS

Did you know that there are a lot of people out there who sit in their offices or homes and read blog posts out loud?

I'm one of these people, and nothing is worse than reading something out loud and not really getting a feel for how the blogger is trying to sound.

I like to write exactly how I would speak, and because I write fairly consistently, you are probably able to get a feel for how I would speak. We'll get more into writing like you would speak in a later chapter, but for now I'd like to talk a little bit about passion and desire.

It's your passion and desire that you want shining through your blog posts. Not only do you want people to be able to understand what you are saying, but also having absolutely no doubt in their mind that you are passionate about what you are talking about.

Sometimes you will find posts where you actually do learn something, but nothing else comes from the visitor because the post didn't sound enthusiastic at all. If it doesn't sound like you are interested in what you are writing about, and if it doesn't sound like you have a desire to make sure people understand what you are talking about, then you shouldn't expect people to desire to comment.

What you give is what you get.

It's true in most cases. If you write a ton of crappy blog posts, and don't care much about what you write, then you can expect little to no visitors, spammy comments, and no further interaction from the people who are visiting your blog. But then, if every post you write contains valuable info, is consistent, easy to understand, and transparent that you are passionate about the subject, then your blog will succeed much further beyond what most other bloggers accomplish.

48

Highlight Other Bloggers

This is a fun little strategy that I've seen people use for both blogs AND books.

It has a few advantages, and is extremely easy to do. You will have to create some content, but most of it is already written for you.

First, I'm going to tell you how I found out about this - it actually wasn't from blogging, it was from book authoring. When I wrote my first book, I started to look at the successes of other books in my niche, and came across a few books that had a list of 20 different authors.

I thought, "How could a book have 20 authors? No one will get paid anything!" But then, when I dove in a little deeper, and contacted the publisher, I found out that the book was actually written, created, and published under on person, and this person is the only one collecting revenue from the book.

He wasn't stealing content either. The only thing he was "stealing" was name recognition. For this one book example, the "author" contacted 20 different entrepreneurs, asked them to include about 1,000 or 2,000 words (could even be taken straight from their blog), and then he compiled all of them together, wrote a quick preface/intro, and PUBLISH.

But then I found something else out. The reason this book was becoming so popular so quick was because when people searched for any of these popular entrepreneurs' names, this very book would show up in the results, usually high on the list.

So then I took this to blogging. And BAM - other people were already doing it, and having success with it, and now I'm sharing it with you.

This is sort of like blog commenting in a sense that you are ethically stealing.

Basically, you are going to create a blog post that highlights one ore more other bloggers. Maybe it's a huge post that highlights 5 or 10 bloggers, or maybe it's a shorter post that highlights just 1 blogger.

The length doesn't really matter as much as the names of the people you include. Make a list of all the names of bloggers in your niche (or even a similar non-exact niche). Then, read some of their blog posts. Finally, make a blog post about a combination of the strategies that they are teaching, or a combo of the types of things they talk about, and in your blog post, include the name of the other blogger. Highlight them, show them off, tell people how cool they are.

When you start to blog about important people in your industry, people will find your blog when searching for their names, because your blog and content relate to the content that this person creates as well.

49

Respond To ALL Thoughtful Comments

Notice I don't say respond to ALL comments. I say respond to all THOUGHTFUL comments.

Some comments are simply rubbish, and aren't worth responding to. Some comments are spam or blatant website promotions. Go ahead and delete these if your spam filter didn't pick them up.

But most of the time when someone comments, they are actually interested in you and your blog, and you need to show some interest in them as well!

As we've discussed plenty throughout this book, interaction is one of the big keys to blogging success. So once you have the interaction from someone else, it's time to interact back!

I mean seriously, I've seen so many blogs that work so hard on getting people to not only come to their blog, but also comment on multiple posts, and then they don't even respond to any comments or thank anyone or give any extra value.

Again, you only need to respond to the thoughtful comments. If 100 people are saying "cool post", you don't need to write 100 responses saying "thanks". Instead, only respond to the people who initiate a conversation, and other people will take notice, and begin to write more meaningful comments on your blog.

People love to be loved, and care about being cared for. Take care with your commenters, and most will be happy and enthused to write more comments in the future, because they know you are an actual nice person who wants to help, interact, blog, talk - basically they know you are THERE.

50

Talk Directly To Your Audience

YOU need to do this. YOU YOU YOU!

Notice that throughout this book, I've really just been having a conversation with you. If someone asked me what my favorite blogging tips and strategies were, I'd immediately start listing off a lot of what I cover in this book. So that's how I wrote it, as if I was having a conversation with YOU.

When you talk directly to your audience, you give them a sense of personality, a sense of a human on the other side of that screen.

This is more than just responding to comments, more than just writing consistently, more than being passionate. If it doesn't look like you care about your audience, your audience won't care about you either.

Stop it with the "you guys". 99.9% of the time, it's not a group of men sitting in front of a computer reading a blog post, so don't call your visitor "you guys".

Instead, focus on YOU. You can do this, you can do that, you do this next, you have success, you talk to me, I talk to you, you should comment, you should have a conversation with me. YOU YOU YOU.

I like to use a little trick my mentor taught me years ago... Instead of laying your blog post out, and just writing, you should lay out what you want to write about, figure out the questions or problems you want to answer and solve, and then pretend that a friend asked you the question, and your blog post is your answer.

Just make your blog posts sound like they are there for one person and one person only: the visitor that is currently reading that piece of content.

51

Share Your Own Experience To Be Unique

Some people just can't stand reading article after article of a blog without really knowing who the blogger is.

You can change this by sharing your own experiences on your blog. You'd be surprised at what sorts of experiences you can share that actually tie in with your own niche.

And I mean heck, if you are going to be blogging hundreds of posts, you BETTER have some sort of experience within the niche your blog is in.

If you made certain mistakes in the past that you wish you hadn't, you can share those experiences with your visitors in order to help them avoid making the same mistakes you did. You can also share your own inspiring experiences, funny experiences, maybe even just a simple experience you had that ties in with what it is you are writing about on your blog.

People appreciate bloggers who go that extra mile to get personal and be personable.

Besides sharing your own experience, let me take a minute to tell you the importance of some of these tips when combined:

You should already be coming up with your own strategies for combining two or more of these strategies. You can share your own experience, write consistently, add a "tweet this link" a few times throughout your post, add a poll, ask a question - And when you combine a lot of these simple little tips and strategies together, they start to work as a unit.

We'll talk more about automation later in the book, but you should start to think about which tips and strategies will work for your blog, which ones won't, and which ones you can combine in order to get maximum blog success leverage.

52

Over Value, Over Deliver, 99% Rule

I just wanted to include a little chapter in here about overdelivering, and always giving more value than you can possibly think.

Have you ever heard of the 99% rule? Some call it 80/20, some 90/10, I go with 99/1.

There are a few different ways to describe these rules, but for me, the 99% rule means giving away 99% of your best content, and leaving out 1% to use for products, e-books, courses, coaching, interviews, etc.

Even if you don't yet have products or ebooks, you should still always be overdelivering, and giving your visitors more than they want, more than they ask for, but EXACTLY what they need.

99% doesn't mean give away 99 tips like this book - that just happens to be how this book is laid out. I of course have been doing my best to overdeliver, and give you everything I have.

You want people to read your blog posts and say, "You should charge people for this info". You want your competitors reading your blog posts and getting pissed off because your free content is better than their paid content!

Only good things can come from overdelivering on value. It's one of those things that you say "yeah yeah, I know", but in fact it's something you should really take some time to think about. Think about what more you could possibly do and give to make people like, share, and talk about you, your content and your blog more.

53

Ask Your Readers A Question

Have you ever been asked a question at the beginning of a blog post, and answered it either out loud OR in your mind?

Whether you answered yes or no, you just proved my point.

You can actually take "popular" YouTube vloggers for instance (they aren't the most entrepreneurial, but they do some things right) - Take a look at vloggers on the top 100 list. What do you notice about a majority of the videos that are posted to these channels? The answer is, they almost always have some sort of question to ask their viewers. And the funny thing is, no matter how stupid or wild the question, they will get THOUSANDS of responses.

Same thing goes for blogs.

Sometimes people don't leave comments and don't interact with you, because they don't know what to say. They don't want to leave a comment saying "thanks, nice article", because it's just not a worthwhile comment. But, if you ask them, "What is your own experience with [insert the blank]?", you will almost always get a larger response.

You can literally ask a question at the beginning and end of EVERY single one of your blog posts. If someone wants to answer, they will, and if they don't, they won't - there is no disadvantage to asking a question.

Let's say your blog post is an informational/review post about a certain product, digital or not. You can ask one question at the beginning of the post, "Have you ever heard of this product/bought this product?", and then one at the end, "Do you know of any similar products?".

What about a "how to" post, or tutorial? - You can ask a question at the beginning, "What types of [things] will you use this [info] for?". Then, another at the end, "What other tutorials do you want to see in the future?".

You can come up with questions to ask your audience for all your posts, and even if they give you one-sentence answers in the comments, at least you are getting more interaction.

Don't think search engines pass up on comments. A lot of the time, search engines will read tags, comments, external URLs in comments, how many comments there are, how recently they were posted, and tons more.

When you get more comments, it helps the human and the visitor - and most of all, helps you and your blog.

54

Positioning Yourself As The Expert

"OMG dude, I'm not an expert, and doesn't everyone HATE experts and gurus?"

If that's your attitude, then I'm sorry, you will never be successful. You see, there's a difference between 'experts/gurus' and 'problem creators'. Okay, I'm sure I can think of a better term than "problem creators", but that's exactly what some of these 'gurus' are.

But the thing is, no matter how much they say they are an expert or a guru, they just aren't. And by problem creator, I mean those people that tell you that you suck, that you are doing everything wrong, that their product will make you rich, successful - they call themselves gurus and experts, but their not either - more like deception artists.

The type of expert that I'm talking about is not perfect, but either has done more or knows more than the audience they create content for.

It's all about experience and knowledge.

Personal experience is obviously the best, because you've been there. You can really explain things in much greater and more valuable detail when you've actually "done it yourself".

Knowledge is also great, especially because you don't have to have 'been there, done that', you just have to know the info and present it in a creative way to your readers and visitors.

Research information, then present it in a new, valuable way. You can even interview experts and gurus and post the text to your blog. More people will associate you as an expert because of your "associate" with experts on YOUR blog.

Just be the "go to blog", and you'll become an expert before you know it yourself.

55

Claim Authorship Of Articles FIRST

This is actually something that not everyone does, but you see it all the time.

Go to Google, type in "how to" and then any keyword after that. It's not just how to articles, but I find people claiming authorship of those articles more often. As the organic search results pop up, you'll notice that some articles/results (usually there is at least one on the first page) have an image of someone next to the result.

Anyone can do this! ANYONE! Well, first you need a Google+ profile.

Right now the URL to set up authorship is: https://plus.google.com/authorship (but of course this can change at any time).

Google Authorship puts a face to your content.

When you claim authorship of your blog and your articles, your Google+ profile image will show up next to every article you have written!

Now when your image shows up next to your article description (when someone searches in google), you will get more views, and more INTERACTION because the article and blog already looks and feels more personal before they even get to your blog.

When you can convince someone that you are both personal AND professional BEFORE they start to read your content, you're 10 steps ahead of everyone else. I hope you're monetizing! ;)

56

AUDIO ON BLOG - PODCAST?

Okay, you might be thinking, podcast? I can't run a podcast!

Guess what? You don't HAVE to manage a podcast to have audio on your blog. That's right, so many people have the misconception that to have audio on a blog, it MUST be a podcast.

The truth is, you can record your voice, make it an mp3, post it as a download in a blog post, and whalah! - You now have audio on your blog!

Getting into audio is good for many reasons.

Sure you can podcast. Sure you can do it the 'paid way' or the 'free way'. It's so easy to setup a simple podcast nowadays, that it would be wrong to lead you in a specific direction in this book. If you want a podcast, go set one up - most websites that have a podcast service give you detailed instructions (and sometimes even COURSES) on how to get started.

But it doesn't have to be a 'podcast' necessarily. It can just be AUDIO.

When people can hear your voice, it obviously adds way more personality to your blog. It ALMOST feels like you're right there (video is better, but audio is great too!).

If you have a MacBook, you have all you need. Basically, you just need a microphone (macs have them built in), a recording tool (mac has garageband, and you can get Audacity for free for PC users), and a blog!

Record ANYTHING you want. Export it as a .wav OR .mp3 file. Upload it to either your Wordpress media library or your file manager (FTP). Then, make a new blog post with a download link to your audio. And if you want them to play and listen to it on your blog, there's plenty of Wordpress (and other CMS) plugins that you can install on your blog for free to place an audio player on your blog.

Just get that audio on your site, it helps. As you'll notice, the more different types of media you have on your blog the better (PDFs, mp3s, articles, videos, slideshows, presentations, podcasts, etc.).

57

Videos On Blog - Vlogging?

I touched on vloggers before, but I'm not talking about updating people on what's in your purse or what you ate for lunch, or the party you went to last night.

I'm talking about providing extra value, giving a sense of personality, communication and interaction, and providing yourself with an extra way of getting visitors to your blog.

A vlog can be about anything, and in any format you choose - but it MUST be a video.

There's no one specific way of doing a video for your blog. Just look at the written content you already have on your blog. If you have your own unique voice, it probably shows in your writing. So, instead of writing it (or in addition to writing it), say it in a video.

Videos can bring in lots of new visitors (from the various video sites you upload your videos to), and will also give the visitors you already have on your blog more value.

Your videos can be short or long, or both. It doesn't matter much, as long as you are getting them uploaded consistently. If you wrote an amazing article - let's say a full review of the new Kindle - instead of just posting the text to your blog, you can also talk about it in your own words in a video. You can then upload your video to multiple video sharing websites, as well as YouTube - then, use YouTube's embed code to post the video to your blog post, and then include a link to your blog post in ALL of the video descriptions for the multiple video sites you uploaded to.

Again - it doesn't matter what type of video it is - just make one! You can even make a 20 or 30 second quick video telling people ABOUT your blog post or content you want them to view or see. Get it? You can either provide extra content in your video, OR you can provide little to no content in the video, and just promote another post you made.

The more videos you upload, the more back links you can get to your blog (and you know how much search engines LOVE back links!) - This also allows you to get personal with your readers, and turns your READERS into VIEWERS. It's always good to have different types of content on your blog and pointing to your blog, and video is the easiest and most lucrative way of getting that job done.

58

Create And Sell A Product!

As you may have noticed, some of these tips and strategies are more time consuming than others.

Don't worry if you can't complete all 99, this list is here to show you the possibilities, and to allow you to choose what is right for you and your blog right NOW.

Some bloggers have products on their blog, but most don't. My question is... Why the hell not?

Seriously, you have GOT to get a product on your blog! Not only will you make some money (and MORE if you do it right), but you will also appear more influential and important because you not only give away great info, but you SELL info, and OTHERS BUY IT!

I'm not able to give you step-by-step instructions on product creation, as that's a topic for a completely different book - but here are the easiest AND most popular forms of products you can sell on your blog:

- E-Book - Yep, the easiest of them all. Type up some good content in a Word document, include links to your blog and great value, add some pictures, maybe some bonus chapters, export/save your doc as a PDF, and you have yourself an E-Book.

- Audio Program - Once you know how to do this, it's even easier than an e-book. You don't even have to write anything! Well, I'd suggest writing a quick outline of what you want to talk about, then just talk. Split up your audio into multiple sections (5 or 10, even 20), and sell it as a complete audio program/package.

- Membership Site - It could be pay-once, pay-monthly, pay-yearly, whatever you want. A membership site works great because you can put literally ANYTHING in the members area. People buy "access" to the members area, where you can include protected articles, audio, video, PDFs and other downloads, bonuses, and this is also great because you can add extra bonuses later and even promote your new and upcoming products to your members.

So besides making the product, how do you sell it?

It's easier than you think... If you are on a super-tight budget, just use a PayPal buy button, and use PayPal to send your buyers their digital product.

You can also join companies like ClickBank or JVZoo or other companies like them - Sometimes you will have to pay a one-time fee to get your product listed, while other sites will never charge you an upfront fee, however they will take something like 5 or 10% from each sale (which doesn't matter, since you don't have to physically send anyone anything or even talk to anyone!).

Just get into product creation, even if it is small. Compile some of your most popular blog posts, add more value to them, turn some of it into audio, maybe even video - make it a product, and SELL!

59

It's Not A Blog, It's A Business

Since we just talked about products, it's important that you understand one thing - your blog is your business.

Now, I'm not saying your blog should be the only asset of your online business, but it should definitely be a big part of what you are trying to accomplish in life and in business.

Business doesn't have to be boring, and it doesn't have to be hard! But you must take into consideration that when your blog gets more popular, the cost of running your blog increases. More email subscribers means more money out of your pocket too.

Some people go into blogging as a hobby, and then have to quit because they were spending hundreds and thousands of dollars each month just to keep their site or blog up and running.

You must treat your blog like a business. Create a product, implement more than one affiliate program, give yourself multiple streams of income.

Don't think you're going to get a million visitors a month, and all of a sudden people will just want to give you money. It takes time, it's a process, most people fail...

I've always liked the term "daily consistent action". When you take action every single day, whether it is blogging, writing, marketing, product creation, promotion, link building - it all helps, especially when you do it over and over.

10 links today, 10 more tomorrow, and keep going - then in 4 months you have 1,000 back links. Same with content - instead of posting once, post daily (at least weekly).

So many peoople only spend a couple hours (or less) on their blog - and then they wonder why they aren't making the big money like these other guys and gals having success. Name 1 business (job) where you can make $1 million in a year by working 1 hour here, 2 there, 1 later on. You can't... You MUST work on your blog as if it is your business - because in reality, it is your business.

60

KEEP YOUR BLOG IN ONE NICHE

You search something, you find an article on a blog, you want to know more about that topic. You look around the blog, and can't find anything else about that topic, in fact you were looking for "blogging tips" and there's articles about "fishing", "makeup", and "politics" on the same page!

Of course, that example is very farfetched, but you get the idea. When someone comes to your blog to read an article, watch a video, listen to you speak, they will probably want other content related to what they just received.

That's why it's important to define your niche from the beginning, and stick with it.

If you have a lot of different wild interests, make more than one blog. You can't expect to have consistent visitors if your blog has 10 or 20 different topics and niches.

When you keep your blog related to ONE niche only, you instantly become an "expert" and an "authority".

Would you take me seriously if in my next chapter, I told you about the best way to apply eyeshadow to your face? Absolutely not, in fact you'd probably stop reading.

Well, same goes for your blog! Sure you can have sub-niches and micro-niches on your blog, but keep it to the nichest topic you can (I think I just made up that word, nichest). Instead of having 5 articles on blogging and 5 articles on skateboarding and 5 articles on music, just have 15 articles on the topic you want your blog to be about.

Besides being an authority figure and an expert on your topic, Google will LOVE you. They'll surely take notice of the VERY-closely-related keywords and titles and categories you have on your blog, and they will begin to rank you better for those terms, since YOU are the one who looks like the authority blog.

An easy way to bump past your competitors is to talk about ONLY one thing. I guarantee if you wrote 10 valuable articles every day for the next year ALL on one topic or niche, you will become THE authority in your niche (definitely closer than you were before).

61

Best Content On Homepage

What's on YOUR homepage?

Let me guess, it reads something like this:

"Welcome to MySite.com, where we do [this, that, and that over there too]! Click here for our blog, click here to read about me, and enjoy the content!"

Then there might be a few links to other pages on your website, maybe a little bit about your blog, and that's about it. Some people don't even use their homepages for anything, and it's crazy.

I'm not saying that all blogs receive most of their traffic on their homepage. All I'm saying is, people are going to get to your homepage. It's the first link in your navigation, it's your URL/domain with no extensions or strings, and people who have never heard of your blog before will usually start at home.

Instead of just 'telling' people what your website or blog is about, you should give some more great content away. And not just great content, your BEST CONTENT.

Your homepage should act as your show-off page. If you have a free PDF download (which links to other products, affiliate promotions, or back to your blog), post the download link to your homepage (or at least a link that gets them to the download page).

You can also have dynamic content (as opposed to static content), like a "best blog posts" widget/plug-in. This will automatically show your best 1, 3, 5, 10, 20 (as many as you want) blog posts based on various statistics like views, comments, social shares, etc.

Just begin thinking of how you can highlight your best content on your homepage, as you will get increased return visitors, better ranking, less page bounces (immediately leaving your site after 1 page view), and more money.

62

SHOW TOP COMMENTERS

I love seeing my name as a "top commenter" on a favorite blog of mine. It makes me want to comment even more.

Have you ever been a top commenter on a blog? I hope you know what a top commenter is... Basically, you can use a plugin to show off the people who comment on your blog the most - you can show them off on any page, but I suggest putting it in the sidebar if you have room.

People love being noticed, recognized, and of course promoted. It's no secret that you'll get more interaction on your blog by basically promoting the people who help you out the most by commenting.

In WordPress, there's plenty of "top comment" type plug-ins and widgets. Search, browse, download and install the plugin, or use another service if it is easier on you (some external comment plugins have a 'top commenter' feature built in).

Quick thought: So I just browsed through a few blogs that have 'top comments' in their sidebars. I noticed that some people actually FIGHT to be #1 commenter! It might sound crazy, but so does wanting your stupid YouTube video comment to be voted up haha.

Once you get top commenters shown on your blog, you will basically be ringing the bell to start the fight - not a fist fight, but a fight to be #1. Instead of punches to your face, you'll get comments to your blog - and LOTS OF THEM.

Don't underestimate good old-fashioned rivalry and wanting to be #1 in general. People want to be seen, people want to be heard, people want to be the best, the first, #1!! It only takes a few minutes to set this up, and once you do, you never have to touch it again, and it can bring you some great results.

63

Highlight Best Content In Sidebar

Okay, I've got a couple more tips for what to put in your sidebar, but just know one thing: Just like you shouldn't go on plugin overload, you also shouldn't go on sidebar widget overload.

You only want what is necessary, and if some of these don't fit in with your blog right now, don't use them - there's plenty of other things you could be doing to make your blog more successful.

So, this little widget/plugin/tip is about highlighting your best content in your sidebar.

Again, you can use a plugin/widget to show off your best content in your sidebar (as opposed to mostly having to do it manually on a page like your home page), and your sidebar will automatically update your best content in real time.

But what if you want to highlight content but your plug-in or widget isn't showing it?

Simple - do it yourself! Not everything has to be automated. In fact, you SHOULD do some manual labor in your sidebar - as it's another prime place of blog real estate. Instead of having a widget JUST show links to your best posts, you can also include an image link to a download, or a page on your site, or even to a product of yours or someone elses.

The more great valuable content you show off in your sidebar, the more likely it is for someone to view 2 or 3 or 50 articles of yours instead of just 1.

Also, I'm sure you can already think of a TON of other "best content" to show in your sidebar. This could be any combination of buttons and image links, affiliate promotions, display ads you get paid for each month, regular links, text, free downloads, gifts, and link exchanges.

Get creative with the content you put in your sidebar, and always try to lead the viewer's eyes in the direction you want them to go.

64

Show Recent Content In Sidebar

Not only should you highlight your best content (or most commented content) in your sidebar, but you should also show off your recent content in your sidebar.

You could go with what most people go with - 5 posts. Or, you could show more, but your sidebar doesn't need that many posts. You could even just show your 1 most recent post to get more people clicking on and seeing the content you just most recently created.

Again, this is easy and takes 1 minute with WordPress. I believe WordPress already has the "recent posts" widget installed automatically, so simply drag the widget to your sidebar, and you're done!

You can choose how many posts show up, as well as a title to display above the most recent posts. For some add-on widgets and plugins, you can also choose to show how many comments each piece of content has, as well as other fun little things. Do some testing, see what looks good on your own blog.

Not sure how many posts to show?

If you are really stuck - don't spend too much time on this. If you have LOTS of widgets and content in your sidebar, then only show 5 posts. If you don't have much sidebar content at all, you can show 10 or even 20 posts to fill things up a bit.

Also, if you have 2 sidebars instead of 1, one trick (sort of a trick, but really just a tip) that I use is making sure both sidebars are about the same height. So... if I have content in one sidebar that goes 100s of pixels down past my other sidebar, I'll either switch some content from one to the other, or just add content to the one that needs some.

You might not think this is a big deal, but trust me - you don't want any blank areas on your blog! It just looks unprofessional. ;)

65

Post Interviews With Friends In Niche

This content strategy works well in all niches, and will do your blog wonders.

Have you ever been interested in someone after seeing their blog, product, book, fan page, twitter page, forum, etc., and then searched their name to read more about the person?

Well, there are lots of people who do this on a consistent basis, and when a name is searched in a search engine, one thing that tends to pop up a lot is interviews.

So in a nutshell, you basically contact and make friends/acquaintanceship with a few people in your niche, then ask them if you can interview them, and it would just be by message/email, you send them questions, they send you answers, and my friend, you have yourself an interview.

When you post this interview to your blog, you'll start to notice more people searching for the person you interviewed, and finding your blog because of it. Then of course, if you have good valuable content, they could become future repeat visitors, which is exactly what you want.

This also allows you to position yourself as an expert.

Let's say for instance I wanted to get some traffic to my blog by leveraging a popular blogger's name. John Chow seems like a cool guy, and he makes TONS of money and has millions of visitors!

Now, I don't suggest going for the big fish, but hey, you never know - I mean all you are doing is basically saying "Hey John, my name is Jack, I'd love to interview you - if you don't have time for a live interview, I've included questions that I'm hoping you can answer, and I will post the interview to my blog here."

Anyway, once you get some names BIGGER THAN YOURSELF onto your blog, other people who know these names will begin to associate them with YOU. Very soon, your name will be mentioned alongside the people's names you include on your blog.

I remember the days when I was "ALL ABOUT DAN KENNEDY!" Then, I saw some random guy start posting some things he learned from Dan, as well as an interview on his blog. Before I knew it, anytime I would mention Dan's name, I'd also list off some other people, and this other guy's name would come out of my mouth - simply because this person associated himself with an influential person.

It's not hard - just start sending some emails. Start with the little fish, like your friends and people who look up to you - and then move on to people in your same boat, as well as people a little more successful than you, then keep moving up until you reach the big dogs.

66

CHUNKING YOUR CONTENT

No, not chucking your content, chunking your content.

Other people refer to this as 'stacking' your content, but I like the term chunking - figured I'd tell you both so when someone talks about 'stacking content', you know you've already heard of it (and will hopefully be implementing it).

If your blog is in a tight niche, and you have a lot of related content on your blog, and I mean a LOT, then this strategy works even better, and you can probably do this within the next 30 minutes.

See, this is where some of the other tips and strategies come into play. I told you before that you need to have a dedicated niche that you consistently write for. Keep writing about that one main topic, and once you have enough posts about your topic of choice, it's time to CHUNK IT UP!

This is very literal - You are basically taking your little bits and pieces (blog posts) and chunking them into larger pieces of content.

This could be a super-long article, but would probably work better as a standalone e-book (of course it all depends on how much content you have and how similar the content is to each other).

See your blog post titles? Those are your chapter titles. See the content of the blog posts? That's the content you put in each chapter of your e-book.

HOW LONG DOES IT TAKE YOU TO COPY AND PASTE?

Just go do this right now - if you are really dedicated to blogging, you should already have enough content to make an entire book!

And by the way, if you are still one of those people who think an e-book needs to be 100 or 200 or more pages, you are terribly wrong. I've bought e-books that were only 7 pages long, but the content was valuable enough to get it for $15 or $20.

If you have multiple categories and a LOT of blog posts (like, hundreds), then you can indeed make more than one book. You can sell them, you can give them away as free downloads - you can include back links in your ebooks to your blog, or to another one of your products (think of this chunked content as the front-end, whereas once they enjoy your chunked/stacked content, they'll be more likely to buy something from you if they find you to be an asset to their success).

67

If You Are The Impatient Type...

Blogging takes patience, one of the most difficult virtues to maintain.

However, if you are ever feeling impatient, and want more more more, then please... Do something that will actually HELP your blog.

Most people get too impatient too quickly, then follow one push-button strategy until their head hurts when they have no increase in visitors. Or, they'll focus on social media too much, and not on the blog content.

Of course it's about adding value, but it's more than that. Don't do something online just for the sake of doing it. Always keep a look out for things that can actually make your blog more successful.

A good choice was buying this book. I strive to offer you tips, strategies, and thoughts about how to make your blog successful. And while it "shouldn't stop here", you also shouldn't go out looking for the 'next best thing', or again - push button crap (unless YOU have proven that it already works - not the sales guy or actor in those videos haha).

It's hard to say right now what exactly you should do first. Every blog is different, and every blogger is different. Some spend way too much time trying to promote one piece of content when they could be creating new content! Some people create too much low-quality content, when they should focus more on creating a few PILLAR pieces of content that they can get more visitors to.

Just make sure you think about this: Before you do a task, buy a product or book, or get ready to make your blog more successful - actually make sure it is going to benefit you.

And one more thing - Just because you can get some quick visitors to your blog from doing some facebook promotion on a lowsy post doesn't mean it's the BEST way to use your time. You may want to go ahead and chunk some content together to create an e-book, and although you might not get the direct visitors or 'success' right away, this is still beneficial because it will bring you more success in the future.

68

Blog About What Others Already Want

Being unique is great, but talking about subjects that hardly anyone is interested in is blog suicide.

Sometimes, you just have to give people what they already want. You can find this out quicker than you think.

What is your blog about, what niche is it in? Where do people go to get answers? Where do people go to ask questions?

When you know what your audience already wants, all you have to do is create it, then tell them about it. This really gets rid of they hypey/salesy nonsense, and allows you to just tell them you have their answer, without telling them they "MUST SEE THIS" or "NEED THIS OR THEY WILL FAIL".

How to know what your audience ALREADY WANTS:

What's your favorite forum? Your audience asks questions ALL DAY LONG in forums. Now, you COULD answer it directly in the forum - OR you could answer the question on your blog in the form of an article, a video, audio, book, etc.

Since you know others are already asking about this, you know that even more are searching for the answer as well. And if YOUR blog post is their direct question, and gives them a full valuable answer, you can be sure that these people will love you, because again, you are giving them exactly what they already want.

So what else? Ask/answer sites can give you good insight into your niche. Other bloggers and blogs and websites in your niche can give your audience what they want too. How about YouTube videos? YES! Check out what others are making videos about - and look at the comments!

Not just YouTube video comments, but ANY comment online. If someone else has created content related to your niche and topic, find out if people still have questions, because they usually do. Someone could make a 15 minute GREAT video, and although you might think the video 'definitely' answered everyone's questions, you will notice that there are still people who want to learn more about a specific topic, or tip, or strategy, or more about anything.

Right now, I want you to open up a Word document. Title it "Content That People Already Want". Keep this document in a safe place. Then, whenever you find out exactly what someone wants from your niche, add it to the list, and you'll have content literally for the rest of your life.

69

Publish Your Good Content, Promote Your Best Content

Any good content you have, long or short, no matter what type (text/audio/video) - you should always publish. Get it out there if it's good!

But you shouldn't be promoting ALL of your content at once, or people could get a case of information overload.

Of course you want all of your content to be heard, and you should tell people about each piece of content you create, but you shouldn't have massive promotions for random stuff on your blog.

If you have an article that gets 5,000 views a month, and gets dozens of new comments monthly, and you have a clear CTA telling people to buy something from you at the end of it, then you need to be promoting this big time!

This is why stats and analytics are important - it shows you what's doing well, what's not, and what you should be promoting more in order to get the most bang for your buck on your blog.

I like to think of it like this: If someone finds your twitter account, your facebook page, your YouTube video, etc., where do they go next? Where exactly do your links point back to? What content are you highlighting and what links are you promoting in order to get people to your blog?

If you have tons and tons and tons and tons and tons and tons of crap (lots of tons), people will click on some random link (since most people make quick decisions when it comes to small things like this) and will get to just another piece of content on your blog. Now this isn't to say that your content isn't valuable - in fact, I hope ALL of it is valuable. But we're talking about success here. If you want to be successful, start to promote your VERY BEST CONTENT. Instead of sending people "wherever", send people somewhere specific that will not only offer them tons of value, but will also give a chance for them to subscribe to your email list, buy a product, click on your ads, follow your social streams, and become a repeat visitor.

70

Answer Questions Directly From Blog Readers

And don't just answer questions personally behind the scenes, answer questions on your blog.

You might think this to be a useless strategy, maybe for the reason that it's not a good use of content.

However, I tend to disagree, let me tell you why...

As you've already learned, you can find exactly what your audience already wants by searching through forums, other blogs, videos, ask/answer sites - but there is an EVEN EASIER WAY to get great content on your blog.

Have you ever been asked a question via email about a piece of content of yours, or even just about your niche and topic in general?

It could even be a question asked directly to you on facebook, twitter, phone even! Besides directly answering the person's question, don't you think others could benefit from this answer as well?

DING! <-- That was the bell that says you just had a breakthrough. No? Think about it, or read on...

Instead of spending 5, 10, 20 minutes or longer answering a question for just one person, you can instead reach 100s, 1,000s, MILLIONS of people by answering the question publicly.

Not only does this give you EXACT and VALUABLE content you can put on your blog, it also shows that you are personal with your audience, and that you really care.
In your post, or video, or audio, you can also say "one of you had a question.. so..." -

When others see that you answered one of THEIR questions, they feel like they are on the same level as you, like you are equal, that you CARE. It's more important than you think, and that's exactly why I included it here.

71

CREATE EVERGREEN CONTENT

EVERGREEN, I just love this word.

Let me break down the word first. EVERGREEN = EVER GREEN = ALWAYS GREEN = ALWAYS GOOD TO GO

So evergreen content just means content that is always fresh, always good to go, always sellable and readable.

Later on I'll talk to you about PILLAR content (which is similar to evergreen), but for now let's focus on the different types of evergreen content.

How do you make content that is always good to go, always relevant?

Well... What stands the test of time?

This book has TONS of evergreen content in it. It also has some content that is not evergreen. Who knows, by the time you or someone else reads this book 10 years from now, YouTube could be gone! Strategies change, the market changes, but the fundamentals will always remain evergreen.

"Google backdoor hack" - hahaha totally NOT evergreen. Every "hack" I've bought into or tried has been proven to work for about 2 or 3 weeks, then Google changes everything and the "hack" doesn't work anymore.

"How to get motivated" - this is 100% EVERGREEN! Now of course, if 'getting motivated' in your mind means using a google backdoor hack, then we're on 2 completely different pages. But if motivation to you means "setting goals, using negatives as positives, and consistently moving forward", then you can bet your bottom dollar that this information can be used 100 years from now!

START CREATING EVERGREEN CONTENT NOW!!!

Some people think if they create 1 blog post a day, in 3 years they'll have over 1,000 pieces of great content. But in 3 years, how many of your articles, audios, and videos still have traction, still mean something, still work? Again, you would be surprised. Depending on what type of content you blog about, you could have 50% evergreen, 20% evergreen, or like I've seen mostly - 5% or less evergreen.

This also goes with always making sure the tasks you do each day for your blog will generate results for you now AND in the future. Don't be one of those people that complains in 5 years when none of your content matters anymore. Instead, start creating content that people will still be sharing on twitter and facebook 10 years from now (or tuushare and faceme - considering twitter and facebook might be gone in 10 years - but your content won't be gone!).

Heck, if you are REALLY new to blogging, and haven't created THAT many posts yet, or haven't been THAT successful yet - you should just go ALL OUT with evergreen content. Then you can laugh in 20 years when your content is still shared around the world, while millions of other blogs and businesses have failed within just a few years.

72

Write Like You Speak, Or Dictate

As I've told you before, I write like I speak.

When you write like you speak, your written content feels more like a conversation, and allows your visitor to get a sense of how you would speak if they were right in front of you.

Who cares if there are missspellings, who cares if you use 3 dots instead of a comma, who cares if you swear or actually write out "haha" or use emoticons and smileys? If it establishes a new sense of personality in your writing, you'll find that more people will read your entire posts, more will comment, more will get to know you, more will read your other posts, and so on.

And the only thing better than writing like you speak is actually SPEAKING! You can either use a free dictation software (I use a paid one, and I admit the paid dictation programs are 10x better than the free ones), OR you can actually just speak right into a microphone, and transcribe it yourself or outsource a handful of articles at a time to someone on an outsourcing website.

Guess what else you can do with these recorded audios? Podcast baby! And not even a podcast, but audio in general. You can make it into a YouTube video, you can post your audio elsewhere, you can stack and chunk your audios and sell them as a standalone product later on.

But back to dictation and writing like you speak...

Just a note - For most dictation software, you must say words like "comma" when you want a comma, "period" when you want a period, and a thousand other things - on the one that I own (Dragon Dictate), you can actually add your own words like "Jack Email Signature", and it will type out whatever you set that word to be.

When you can dictate your words right from your mouth, it makes it SO easy to create content. If you use software where you must say "comma" and "period", you obviously can't record it as a podcast or direct audio, because it would obviously sound very weird to people listening. However, the joy of just speaking right into the microphone allows you to use it as an audio, a video, as well as an article. Of course, YOU will have re-type what you spoke, so that's the only extra step.

If anything, at least try this for your next 5 articles. You may get used to it, and use it all the time. Just try dictating, and really - make some audios and videos from it, and then write your blog posts from your audio (or again, outsource).

73

Create Social Accounts For Your Blog

Plenty of people just skipped this chapter all-together, because they think they are social media masters.

Don't be one of those people that thinks a facebook page and a twitter account will do it anymore.

In my book, 99 Ways To Flood Your Website With Traffic, I talk a lot about social media, and how sometimes you have to be in a million places at once.

You don't have to use 100 social networks every single day, but at least set up an account at various social networks. It gives you more social backlinks, profile backlinks, and sometimes you'll get some extra traffic from these social sites.

The more you put into social media, and the more personal you are on social media outlets (instead of making it a total pitch fest), the more you will benefit from it.

You can find a list of 100 different social networks and streams and outlets and websites, then setup 100 profiles, then add a link to your blog on EVERY account. Then, post all your new content links to these social networks. Build relationships and add value to other people, and most of all - show that you care!

Add your profile picture, brand it the same on ALL your networks. And whatever the different networks call it - following, friending, liking, whatever - add people, follow people, friend people, SHARE with people.

Think about it this way - You could definitely do about 5 minutes of work on facebook and twitter, and could add dozens and dozens (and maybe even 100 or more) friends, as well as follow hundreds of people (you can follow up to 2,000 people if your twitter account has less than 2,000 followers). These create connections, you know that.

But now what if you did that same thing on 98 other social websites? Add/follow/friend/share/subscribe - do that 100 times on 100 networks (add 100 friends, follow 100 people, subscribe to 100 people, just 100 on each network), a lot of things happen:

First, you get backlinks. Search engines love backlinks, especially social links. So, more back links, better rankings.

Next, you get intant traffic. There's no doubt in my mind that you will get a nice little spike in traffic (unless you already get tens of thousands of visitors per day already). Why? Because 100 follows/friends/adds/subscribes/shares on 100 different websites means 10,000 brand new chances for your blog and your content to be seen.

Besides the instant traffic, if you make a strong connection with even a few people, they will share your blog and content with others, and this can give you viral sustainability.

Is this important? Yes. Should you do this before EVERYTHING else? Yes AND no. Yes because you should want to make your blog more successful, and NO because your blog might not be ready to share. It's better to first have good content and your entire blog set up (with share buttons, opt-in boxes, products, etc.), because then when you do this initial social blast, as well as future social blasts to all your new networks, you have a MUCH GREATER chance of getting more shares, more visitors, more repeat visitors, more sales, more money, more success.

74

Multiple Affiliate Program Integration

You might not want to create a product. You might not want to set up an ad-buying program on your blog.

But do not pass up on making more money through easy affiliate commissions!

It's very easy to make money with affiliate marketing on blogs as long as you have a high-converting highly-relevant offer or opportunity that YOUR audience wants.

The biggest problem most have is the actual products they promote. Too many just go for products that give you hundreds of dollars per sale, but maybe your visitors don't want to pay that much. On the other hand, if you promote products that are super-cheap, you'll make very small commissions.

It also comes down to what the product is - Does this product actually have value for your audience? Do they really want it and need it?

It all comes down to one thing: testing.

First, at least start promoting something. Go with your gut, and get an affiliate ad on your blog, for a product that you believe will actually benefit the visitors of your blog. If you don't know what affiliate marketing is, basically you get some sort of a "coded link" (ClickBank calls it a hop link, others call them tracking links), and when you share the link (could even be an image link), and someone clicks it AND buys the product, you get a commission for the sale. Some offer 10% and less (Amazon right now hehe), some anywhere from 25% - 75% (like ClickBank/JVZoo right now), and some even 100% (Empower Network).

But once you get that first affiliate ad on your site (put it in the sidebar, or try below each post - use a simple WordPress plugin to show content underneath your posts), you should be checking out more affiliate systems and websites. Do some testing, ask some of your inner circle close friends and followers what they think about various products. This will give you the edge, and will allow you to figure out what products work best on your blog.

75

STEALING OTHER'S BLOG TRAFFIC

You aren't really stealing anything, but once you start getting hundreds of people flowing into your site after a couple hours of work, you'll think it's stealing.

What I'm talking about is ethical, and is commonly used on blogs and videos.

It's about blog commenting. But not the old spammy kind, the new value-adding kind.

Usually when people tell you to comment on blogs, they tell you to write the same type of "nice post!" comments, some even give you templates to work with.

If you are going to use this strategy to steal other people's blog traffic, please make sure you are actually adding value in your comments.

I'm not saying you MUST read every word of the article or watch every second of the video, but at least skim it, see if you can find any gold nuggets, actually TRY to learn something new.

Then, when you write your comment, you are able to write a full sentence or two about what you thought of the full article, and maybe be able to add your own value or extra tip, or some inspiring thoughts.

HERE'S THE SECRET: You want to SELL people on clicking your name (which you will link to your own blog) WITHOUT SELLING them on it.

In other words, don't tell them to check out your blog. Instead, show them WHY they should check out your blog.

NEVER talk about your own blog in a comment. Simply provide value and be genuine and nice, and you'll get people clicking over to your blog.

Here's another secret: This isn't super secret, but I don't see many people talking about this. If you really want to get LOTS of traffic from other people's blogs, you need to comment EARLY and OFTEN. This will enable you to become a top commenter, as well as be an early commenter, which on most blogs allows you to be the first comment to show up right after the blog post (it's basically like free advertising). The closer you are to the top, the more valuable and lengthy your comment, and the more you comment, the more traffic you can get.

It's like buying real estate and using the land and housing as rental properties. Get your own content and name and links on 100s of other people's blogs, and basically RENT space on their blog. Except instead of paying them for an advertisement, you pay your TIME to write comments and provide value.

76

DRIP POSTING / POST SCHEDULING

It's shocking that many don't know that WordPress allows you to schedule (or "drip") your posts for the future.

People sell plugins and software for tons of money that does this exact same thing (of course probably with added features) - yet WordPress gives this to you for free.

Drip posting is something you need to do IMMEDIATELY.

This is one of my favorite strategies. Drip posting means you write posts and schedule them for the future, and WordPress can post your content down to the SECOND!

If you do a weekly Friday audio post or article, you can create 4 of them, or 10, or 100 - and then schedule them, and let WordPress drip them over time onto your blog.

Search engines love consistent content, and don't like inconsistent content. Dripping your content on a schedule allows you to bring in consistent rankings, consistent traffic, and almost always builds your audience faster. When people see consistent content from you, and excellent content at that, then they will come back, they will opt-in, they will buy.

If you don't have a drip poster or post scheduler inside your blogging platform, it's not too hard to do it manually. You write all the posts at the same time like the previous strategy, but instead of your articles being posted automatically, you will save your articles in a folder on your computer desktop, OR write all your articles in your blog platform, save them as a draft (some call it "save for later"), and then post them whenever you want (but keep it to some sort of a schedule). Doing this manually isn't bad at all. Instead of having to spend 30 minutes, 1 hour or more to write content each day/week, it just takes you 2 minutes to log in and hit "post" or "publish".

On top of all the benefits I've already listed, scheduling and dripping your posts allows you to do work without really doing work. You can now spend your time on marketing and promoting your new post, getting back links, and sharing it with the world.

77

Monetize Content, Turn Text Into Links

This is one of those things you can do when you're bored. It's time consuming, but can bring your blog lots of money.

When some people think of a successful blog, they might think 100,000 visitors in a month is a lot. But is it really? If you have 200 posts, 10 pages, and other various pages that get counted in stats, that means you probably get less than 1,000 visitors (and probably much less) to each page on your blog, and maybe more on a few popular pages or posts.

Then, you take into consideration that only a few of your pages have true CTAs that allow you to make money from your visitor. If only 5 pages are monetized, you are getting only a couple thousand visitors, which if they convert at 1%, could mean only a few clicks, and probably not even a sale.

In order to truly make money from your blog, you need to monetize ALL of your content.

Again, this is something you can do when you don't know what else to do. It's also something you can do when you don't feel like doing multiple tasks. THIS task will be worth doing, because you know that the more you do it, the more money your blog will make.

I've talked a bit about affiliate marketing before - you promote other people's products and programs, and you get a commission for clicks, sales, leads, whatever that specific affiliate program promises.

But as you've probably noticed, those sidebar ads don't get as many clicks anymore, do they?

People aren't on your blog for the sidebars, they are there for the CONTENT! So... instead of trying to lead them to your affiliate promotions in the sidebar, bring the affiliate promotions to the content!

They don't even have to be blatant promotions. All you have to do is "link up" your text. I'm sure if you have been blogging for awhile, there's a chance you've talked about something related to a product, program, or TYPE of digital 'something' that someone is selling. Do you talk about knitting? There's courses on that you can promote. Do you talk about art? There's TONS of courses, books, step by step programs, and lessons that are sold on the internet. Ever talk about a cool physical product? Use Amazon's Associate Program to affiliate-link keywords that relate to a specific product on Amazon, and make some commissions!

The more links you add throughout your content, the more money you'll make. Think of Wikipedia. How many times have you clicked on a link WITHIN the content of a page? Hundreds, probably thousands or more. YOU can actually get paid for it though when someone clicks and buys.

Remember the math I broke down on 100,000 visitors earlier? With the example I gave, you'd get only a few clicks.

But let's now say that you have EVERY page monetized with at least 10 affiliate/promoted links on each page. Well, from the example of 100,000 visitors, you are now actually getting 100,000 true chances of clicking. And when you have multiple links on each page, the chances are even higher. You'll find that some people click on more than one link.

As you can see, if you put in a little work, you can expect a HIGH raise of income for you and your blog.

78

"Monetized" Section Under Content

Besides ads and text links, you can also have a little section underneath your content that makes you money.

Remember when I said it's good to have a clear CTA at the bottom of the content, as well as an email opt-in form below your content? Well this is another thing you can add below your content.

Like I said before, people are more likely to "go to the next step" once they have just finished reading your blog article. So, you've given them the chance to comment, the chance to sign up to your email list, the chance to read another post, and now you are going to give them the chance to buy a product!

Again, you don't have to make this product. It can be an affiliate promotion, a CPA ad, display advertising, e-books and physical products from Amazon - you name it, you can put it there.

Again, you should find a plugin or widget of some kind that you can use that adds content to the end of your post.

QUICK TRICK (workaround): If you can't find a "display under posts" plugin that works with your version of WordPress, I found that there are some plugins that work on all versions, like some share button plugins - and some of these have options where you can display text/code/anything before and after the share buttons (which can be shown below your post) - SO... all you have to do is add your affiliate links and ads to this little "show this content before share widget/plugin", and your affiliate promotions will now show up above your share buttons and below your post content.

The great thing about using these plugins is that when you want to change anything, it only takes one edit instead of having to change it for every single post.

You can promote one product, you can promote multiple products, they can be links, they can be images. You can even put 6 or 9 or 12 images in some sort of table (search how to make an HTML table, it's easy!), and have a little block of affiliate ads at the bottom of your post.

Finally - Make sure you TEST. If you are getting a lot of traffic, but no clicks on those ads, change it up a bit. If it's all text, change it to images. If there are no clicks on multiple images, try one BIG image with one specific promotion. This just gives you one more piece of real estate, one sign, one last chance to make some money on your blog.

79

THE OUTBOUND LINK STRATEGY (NOTIFY/TRACKBACK)

You've definitely come across this if you are at least a somewhat popular or important blogger (or at least noticed).

You log in to your blog dashboard, and get a notification that says "trackback from: [insert name here]".

This means that another blog has mentioned one of your blog posts in their content, or comments, or somewhere on their blog.

This is an amazing opportunity if done correctly.

Now, not ALL blogs have 'trackback' features in their dashboard or on their blog publicly, but MOST DO.

Trackbacks usually show up either above or beneath the comment section of the blog posts, and include the title of the web page that a link to THAT specific blog post has been published to (trackbacks also show as LINKS - which link BACK to the other webpage).

So, all you have to do is link to other people's blog posts, and they will receive a TRACK BACK.

Here's what that does for you:

- These blog admins will get a notification in their dashboard that a new trackback has been published. If you link to 100 blogs, you will get about 100 bloggers looking at your trackback link (and if it is relevant to their blog, this can open up some big opportunities).

- These track backs create links on the posts you linked to. Link to 100 blog posts, and get about 100 back links (again, this is only if they have track backs enabled).

- This creates a nice back link not only for people coming to your blog directly from the other blog, but also for search engines to spider and rank your website accordingly.

So how do you link to 100 blog posts? Easy... You can do it in just 1 blog post!

Now of course, I recommend you write at least a few posts where you only link to one or two, or a few blog posts from other blogs before you do what I tell you here.

But, here's how to do it in 1 shot: Write a blog post titled something like "100 Best [insert topic here] Blog Articles".

Then, simply find 100 blog posts on other blogs that you can see have other trackback links already, and copy and paste the URLs to those blog posts into YOUR blog post.

You don't have to create any content (besides maybe an intro and outro and CTA) - just find posts, list them as links, and watch the back links appear.

80

Invite Guest Authors and Bloggers

I wouldn't go overboard with this, as you don't want your blog turning into a hosh-posh of someone else's content.

But, inviting other people to be a guest blogger on your blog is a great way to make connections, get more visitors, and become more of the 'go-to blog'.

The reason I say not to go overboard is because most people get this idea, and go too crazy with it, and before you know it they have hundreds of posts that aren't the best quality.

However, I'd say inviting others to be a guest blogger on your blog is a great thing to do, and it only takes a few minutes.

Just set up a page on your website called "guest blog" or "guest bloggers", and explain to people that they can write for your blog, and you'll allow 1 back link and footer info in every one of their posts. Then, include your email so they can send you their submissions. You can then approve and dissaprove these submissions - and the ones you approve only take another minute to post to your site.

This is so easy to do, almost TOO easy, yet many still don't take advantage of this on their blogs.

When you post other's content on your blog, many things can (and usually will) happen:

- The person who wrote the content WILL promote, link, and share the post. They will be proud to have their writing posted on a legitimate blog, and will want their friends and fans to see it.

- You will be seen as someone who has a team, someone who allows others to share their own story, their own thoughts. You look like someone who wants to share, wants to help.

- If the guest blog author becomes popular at ANY point in the future, then when people search for their name, YOUR blog will show up early in the search results, because their name will be on the post on YOUR blog, and search engines will know that it showed up there much earlier, which makes your page more important.

- You get CONTENT, period! Don't overlook this. More content means more traffic, and if you are following many of the other tips and strategies I've provided to you in this book, then you'll convert this traffic into subscribers, leads, and buyers, like clockwork.

Don't be shy, make your "guest blogger" page right now, and allow others to post on your blog - as the main person it benefits is YOU.

81

Guest Post On Other Blogs

Don't stop with inviting people to guest post on your own blog, you should also be guest posting on other blogs as well.

In my opinion, guest posting on other blogs is just as important as having people guest post on your own blog.

You might have heard that guest posting on other people's blogs doesn't do much for you, and although I agree partially, let me give you my take on this...

As I told you in the previous tip, when others guest post on your blog, they will be able to add a back link to their post.

So, instead of just saying "I shouldn't blog on other blogs", you should instead just make sure it actually benefits you.

First, make sure this person allows a back link - if they don't allow a back link or two to your own blog, don't post on that person's blog; There are plenty of other blogs that would be happy to post your links.

Next, make sure you are allowed to include your name as the author of the post. You WANT people to know that you wrote that content. If you are going to spend any time at all on a guest post, you want to make sure you are going to get credit and praise for it, and not just the other blog.

Finally, make sure the blog you guest post on is RELEVANT to what your blog is about, as well as the type of person you are. If you have a tech blog, don't post on an entertainment blog (unless the majority of their visitors are of the tech following). Instead, find another tech blogs to guest write on. You will receive more relevant visitors coming to your blog, and your name will be associated with tech, and not something else.

Final words about guest posting on other blogs: I would say that writing posts on your OWN blog is always more important than writing posts on OTHER blogs. However, if you have lots of posts, and have posts scheduled for the future, and you've got content up the ying yang, then go ahead an do some guest posting - it wouldn't hurt.

82

Participate In Blog Groups

Blog carnivals, blog groups, google groups, yahoo groups, facebook groups, offline groups, email groups, mastermind groups - there are all sorts of groups you can join today, for free!

Participating in blog groups gives you the chance to interact directly with other bloggers. A lot of the time, people in these groups will promote your content, comment on your content, share it with their friends. Sometimes people will even write about you!

Get involved in groups - and get surrounded by people who are like you!

And besides surrounding yourself with people who are like you, surround yourself with people more successful than you.

By surrounding yourself around the right people, you will get to see what they are writing and blogging about. You can see who's creating products, what they are about, what their audiences want, what they need, what they absolutely LOVE. Getting into groups like this allows you to pick up on tricks of the trade - and you'll definitely get a lot of gold nuggets and 'aha' moments.

But on top of being able to get inspiration from successful people who are like you, you are also able to share your own blog posts, products, and promotions with your buddies in these groups. And a lot of the time (especially if you are sharing THEIR content), they will SHARE YOUR CONTENT!

You can join a blog carnival or link group right now. You can then join 20 google groups, 10 yahoo groups, 30 facebook groups, as well as any other forum-style blogging groups online.

This gives you dozens (and sometimes hundreds) of new places you can post your links. You'll get more traffic, more sharing, more social back links, which is ALL good for you and your blog.

Tip about any type of online group: I've found that the more generous you are to others in any group, the more generous people are to you. If you consistently like, share, and comment on other people's posts and promotions in your group, you can expect an influx in the response of your own posts and links. Just always be adding value into other people's lives, and be REAL.

83

PILLAR CONTENT (SIMILAR TO EVERGREEN)

Okay, here we are, pillar content. A few chapters ago, we looked into the world of EVERGREEN content.

Some people describe pillar content and evergreen content as the same thing, but I find them to be a little different.

With evergreen content, you are simply looking to post content that someone can view in 10 or 20 or 30 years, and still get the same effect, same results - nothing needs to be changed.

Most pillar content is also evergreen, but your pillar content is what really sells your blog to your visitors, and can really boost your ranking big time.

When I think of pillar content, I think of the posts that are INFLUENTIAL. You know those posts that you read, and you say "there's nothing more I need to read on this specific subject - this explained it ALL!" - THAT is what you are going for.

But besides giving people everything, you also want them to gain enough interest and curiosity in you, your blog, and your other posts.

Another important aspect of pillar content is that it should explain, talk about, and LINK TO other posts and pages on your blog.

One example of a piece of pillar content could be a post titled "How To Get Motivated, Every Day". Then, within this post, you have sections that explain a few different ways of getting motivated. Then, also inside the post, you link to other pages on your blog that talk about motivation. If you talk about being stressed or getting depressed, make sure you have another article to link to that talks about those subjects in more detail or specifically.

And don't think once you've written your post, that you can't add to it later!

When you add more posts and content to your blog, you should go back to your big pillar posts and add links to your new posts and pages on your blog. You want your visitors who read these pages to be clicking on your links to read even MORE that your blog has to offer.

Essentially, when someone finds your pillar posts, it means they are looking for LOTS of answers. No one searches "how to get motivated" if they aren't having problems. They need ANSWERS. If they can't find it on your blog within minutes, they'll hit that 'back' button faster than you can convince them they should stay. But when you provide dozens of links and resources on this page that only link to other places on your blog, you are keeping them around longer, and appear to be the "go-to" resource on the subjects you blog about.

84

A Blog A Day Keeps The Slaps Away

We all hate slaps from Google. And really any search engine or website for that matter.

It sucks even more when all you do is post great content, and still get slapped by the search engines.

I've noticed that blogs that are updated regularly aren't slapped as much or as hard by Google. Of course, there will always be exceptions, but this is a good strategy to follow if you want to stay away from losing all your search engine traffic overnight.

You know it as well as I do - no matter how much we talk about other ways of getting traffic, search engine traffic is always the best, because it is essentially FREE. You aren't paying people to look at your posts, people are FINDING your posts, and it's a great feeling to not have to pay directly in order to get someone looking at your content.

Consistent daily action. That's what it takes to be successful in anything. You've heard it before, maybe so many times that you hate hearing it - but it's true.

Now, I'm not saying that when you start to blog every day, that everything will change and you'll make millions instantly.

All I'm saying is... Think about all the benefits that can come from blogging daily...

- More content.
- More digital 'real estate'.
- More chances to monetize.
- More chances to get your content shared.
- More chances to change someone's life or make someone's day.
- More consistency which shows you are serious about what you do.

There's plenty of more benefits that I'm sure you've even thought of - the point is... if you want a tried and true strategy for gaining exposure and avoiding being slapped or penalized by search engines, blogging daily can help that, more than you think.

And again, this is where post scheduling comes into play. Sure, you might not want to create a bunch of content EVERY DAY. So then do a week's worth of posts in a day! 1 pillar post, 3 semi-long quality posts, and 4 smaller posts or other's videos with your commentary. Just get some consistency in your blog, only good things will happen.

85

A Note On Spinning Article Content

Article spinning was big back in the early Adsense days. People would take one large 3,000 word article, split it up into ten 300 word articles, then "spin" the content to make it original. Each of the 10 articles would be spun 20 times each, giving you 200 articles to post to your blog in less than an hour. Then, those 200 articles would pick up lots of different variations of keywords, bring in search engine traffic, and even if each article only made $1 a day, that gives you $200 per day, which is $73,000 a year, just by creating 1 article.

It doesn't work that way anymore.

Algorithms get tougher and more in depth, and Google's Ark keeps sending out animals to destroy sites with bad content!

So does article spinning work anymore?

Yes, but it has definitely changed. Most people claim things are "dead" when they don't work the same way anymore. Spinning isn't 'dead', it's just changed. It's those that went with the change and came up with new strategies that continued to profit, while others just stopped because they didn't want to learn anything new.

I would say first of all, no matter what you are spinning, it MUST be your own content. Don't take someone else's content and spin it, then call it your own. It's unethical, and can get you in a lot of trouble.

Instead, write your own 1,000 word article, and spin THAT.

There's a few free article spinners online right now, and the later you read this, the more there will be - so do a quick search!

Then, what you want to do is first put your full 1,000 word article in the spinner, and create 5 unique posts.

Next, split up your article into sections - it can be 2, 3, 4, or even 5 sections. NOTE: The more sections you have, the less words each article will have. I also recommend you vary your spun post lengths to look more natural in the search engines.

But once you split your article into sections, re-spin those mini-articles, yep - 5 times again, each! As you can see, you can soon have 10 or 20 or even 50 articles for you - all with original content, just changed a little to get different keywords in your content (so search engines pick up the different keywords that others are searching for).

NOW THIS IS WHERE PEOPLE GET IT ALL WRONG!!!

Listen up - this is where most people would tell you to post ALL 20 or 30 of these articles to YOUR blog. DON'T DO THAT!

You see... Although the posts are 'unique', if you post too many of the same spun article on one domain, Google and other search engines could pick up on it, and PENALIZE your blog! You obviously don't want that to happen.

And what I'm going to tell you right now isn't just so you don't get penalized - I actually think this helps WAY MORE on it's own:

What you want to do is post all of your spun articles to OTHER places online. Article sites, free blogging sites (blogger, tumblr), sites like squidoo and hubpages, and place that allows you to post content with little restrictions, that also allows you to POST LINKS in your content.

You are going to want to spin your articles more often, so you want to have a full slew of blogs and content hubs that you can post this content to quickly and easily.

Set up 20 blogs on blogger.com - All you need is one google account, and hit the "create new blog" button 20 times, get 20 new titles, and post to all 20. You can spin 1 article 1 time and have content on ALL of these blogs. Same goes with squidoo and hubpages - create 1 account, and write TONS of content (lenses and hubs). Articles sites - same thing. Have 1 account on multiple article and content sites, and submit your spun articles once to each site.

This not only allows you to have content online that you can call your own, but gives you BACK LINKS - this is the prime motive for these spun articles. These back links raise your rank in the search engines, and also gives you DIRECT visitors to your blog. Your back links can go straight to an article on your blog, or even just to your home page!

Now, you might be thinking - "Isn't this spun article content not as high quality as original-written content?"

My answer is... IT DOESN'T MATTER. You aren't publishing this content to get people to say "I like this guy/girl" - in fact you don't even have to post your name or brand anything on these external sites and pages. You want people to search for a keyword, find this content, and then feel like they haven't learned enough, or want more, so then they think, "where should I go next?" - Well, if you have multiple links in this content, there's a high chance they'll say "hmm... let me try THIS link!".

And here's the kicker: If you were just to write one post on your blog titled "How To Get Girls", you would only be targeting people who search for "how to get girls" in search engines. And if there are more popular pages than yours for that keyword, you'll NEVER be found. But, if you have 50 spun articles for that one post, and each one has a different keyword, more people will find these posts. In one article, you can target "how to win your girl's heart", then another can be "how to win MY girl's heart" - those are 2 different keywords, and although they basically say the same thing, they could have MUCH higher or lower competition (this is also where KEYWORD RESEARCH comes into play - go fool around on the Google Keyword tool a bit).

Then you could target your other spun articles like "how to get girls attention", "how to get attention of women", "how to attract women to you", "how you can attract women today" - you get the idea.

You can now have 100s and 1,000s of articles instead of just dozens. They all target the same people, just MORE of them.

86

PLR Content That Works Wonders

PLR means Private Label Rights.

There is also MRR - Master Resale Rights, and lots of other various resale rights content.

Many people disregard PLR content simply because there is so much that is crap. But, give yourself a couple hours to search around, and you can find dozens of great ebooks, courses, audio programs, and other content that would work great for site, AND that you can give away for free!

There are so many things you can do with PLR content.

Just search for any term, plus the world "PLR" or "reuse rights" or "reslae rights". You'll almost always find e-books, audio, video, and other content that you can do whatever you want with, FOR FREE.

And if you want QUALITY PLR content that not everyone can get, you can always join a PLR group or pay for PLR content to be more exclusive.

So what do you do with PLR content?

Well, for this book, I'll talk about PLR E-Books in particular, since that is what's easiest, and what most people use as PLR online.

One thing that's obviously the most obvious is you can directly post the e-book as a free download on your blog. Your visitors will love you for giving them something for free.

You can also make it so that people have to opt-in to your email list in order to get the e-book. This also allows you to get FREE LEADS, who you can give stuff to and sell stuff to later.

Something that most people don't think of is syndicating and breaking up the content.

Remember before how I talked about "chunking" your content into a book? Well, think of this as REVERSE-CHUNKING. Haha, yeah, I created a new word!

You can break up a 40 page PLR e-book into 40 articles. Or, if an e-book has 15 chapters, make each chapter a LONG article. You can post as-is, but I would suggest adding your own value and changing up some of the content.

Another thing you can do is use PLR content as external content to link to your blog. You can use this as-is, or take a PLR e-book, break it into 20 articles, then spin those into 300 or 400 shorter articles. Do you see how many back links and extra content you can have pointing back to your blog?!

One more thing you can do (a little more time involved for this one) is use the content for your own audios and videos - syndication. Learn the content from a book, then make a full video explaining everything in your own words. Or, speak the whole book in your own words into a microphone - when you are done, you'll have hours of audio, which you can split up into sections, and then either giveaway as a package, post to your blog, make a podcast, or SELL IT!

The reality of PLR is that there is just so many opportunities that you and many others are missing out on. Just start thinking outside of the box, and you'll find that there is a LOT you can do with PLR content, and other types of content like this.

87

Micro-Blogging To Boost Readership

We already talked about micro-posts, now let's talk about micro blogs.

If you want to boost readership to your blog, an easy way to do that is to set up dozens of micro-blogs related to your main niche, but have a specific super-tiny-microscopic niche.

You can tie your article spinning in with this strategy as well - and when you do, make sure you set up a VERY SPECIFIC MICRO-NICHE for each blog.

If your main blog is about horses, you should set up 10 micro blogs (use free blogger.com sub-domains), each about a specific type of horse, or specific type of riding, or a SPECIFIC horse's name!

How does this help?

Well as I've said before (in regards to keywords), I'm guessing that you aren't ranking #1 for the main keywords you want on your blog.

Let's keep the 'horses' example for this chapter: You aren't going to get traffic for the search term "horses", it's just way too competitive.

So, besides targeting sub-keywords and micro-keywords and long-tail-keywords on your blog, you can also target VERY SPECIFIC keywords on other content, and link it to your blog.

Let's say you'd like to target people who like horses. Well, is there something VERY SPECIFIC about horses that these people are searching for, which could eventually lead them to your MAIN blog about horses? How about... horse brushes?!

You could set up besthorsebrushes.blogger.com (or something like that), and write (and spin) 100 articles, ALL RELATED TO HORSE BRUSHES ONLY!

There's no doubt in my mind that this blog will get picked up as one of the GO-TO blogs when people search for horse brushes.

I hope you are getting the idea, and I hope that your light bulb is shining bright, because this is golden stuff here! Sometimes you can't get people to your blog because EVERYONE is talking about the same stuff, and so many different things at that! So, pick a very super-micro-sub-niche topic, write a BUNCH of content for it, and link it all back to your main blog. You'll get better rankings, more traffic, and more interaction.

88

Submitting Blog To Directories

Another no-brainer, but many fail to take these steps in their blogging career. This is often a step that is skipped.

This won't make or break your blog, but especially at the forefront start of your blog, it helps to have a lot of backlinks and promotion pointing to your blog.

Now, I'm not going to go too in depth with this, because this is one of those tips that has been heard before - but I will tell you that if you've NEVER submitted your blog to a directory before, and your blog isn't as successful as you want it to be, just do this now.

You are going to want to submit your blog to MANY directories - and yes, it will take time. But it's time well spent, and you only have to do it once!

When you submit your blog to 100s of directories, you get back links, more traffic, more exposure, more promotion, and more FREE advertising. That's the best part, and why you should do it - it's free.

Go run a search for "list of best blog directories" and "list of top directories".

You'll find 100s, and probably 1,000s of directories you can submit your blog to. You will also find services that submit your blog to some directories automatically - DO IT.

Go down these lists, and keep submitting until your fingers are about to fall off. Okay, I'm kidding, but seriously though - get yourself some easy back links and easy traffic. And again, think about your RANKING. When you have 100s of directories linking to your blog, your rank will only get better.

TIP: Try submitting your blog to as many HIGH PAGE RANK directories as possible. Some have page ranks of 2 or 3, and some as high as 6, 7, and 8. You want to submit your blogs to the highest page-rank directories simply because it gives you the best link juice.

89

Put Blog URL In EVERY Signature (THINK)

No, not just email signatures, there are dozens of places to put a signature.

This is exactly why people say "that doesn't work", because they STOP SHORT!

There has got to have been SOMEONE who has told you to place your blog URL in your email signature. But don't stop there!

Here's some other places you can post your link in 'signatures':

- Email autoresponders
- Email broadcasts
- Facebook posts
- Facebook messages
- Twitter messages
- Blog posts
- External content
- Video descriptions
- Any social profile

What most people don't do is post signatures in these places - but why not?

I started to get this idea about a year ago from a buddy of mine. I started to notice when I'd interact with him on twitter, facebook, email, as well as skype - ALL of his messages and forms of communication included the SAME signature - and I eventually clicked on his blog link, simply because I saw it enough times.

Did you know that it can take up to 7 times (or more) of seeing something or hearing something before someone decides to take action on it? The more your signature is out there with your blog link, the greater chance you have at someone clicking on your link and visiting your blog.

Easy way to include your signature everywhere: So obviously, places like facebook and twitter don't have an option to include your signature in every comment, post, or message you send or share.

So... create a text document titled "MY VIRAL SIGNATURE", and include the signature(s) you want to use. Keep this text document handy (on your desktop works great), so any time you communicate with someone online, you are able to copy and paste your signature without having to type it every time.

The best part about these signatures is that it doesn't look like you are saying "CHECK THIS OUT" directly. Instead, people see it as a normal part of any communication - since they see it all the time in blog posts, emails, direct mail, forums, and many other places online and offline. It doesn't even look like you typed the signature yourself, it just looks automated, so no one will tell you to "stop spamming them", they'll just decide whether or not to click on your link.

90

Package Old Content Into Books

This works like content chunking, but is specifically for ebooks.

Some people would rather just download a book instead of reading through 500 different articles to get the same info.

So, why not package a bunch of your old articles into a book? It's not as hard as you think. Here, let me show you.

Now, with content chunking, you can turn your content into books, large articles, audio, video, and other forms of content.

I believe creating e-books is one of the best things you can do for your blog, and you already have TONS of content on your blog that you can use.

Of course you'd want to add more content to the e-book, but you can literally take ALL of your best content and turn it into an e-book.

You can give away the e-book for free, but I'd suggest selling it!

Don't think just because some of the content in the book is already available for free on your blog that people wouldn't pay for it! You are providing the value of your audience being able to GET IT ALL AT ONCE - right here, right now.

We've already talked a lot about this stuff, I just wanted to really drill in your head that you should be packaging old content into books all the time.

Whenever you create new content for your blog, you should also add it to a document you use specifically to add the content to books in the future.

The more content you create for your blog, the more content you'll have for your books - this gives you more of an incentive to blog daily, because you'll know that in a week or two, you'll have ANOTHER book that you can make money from!

And besides selling your book, you can also give your book away for free and make money from affiliate promotions in your book! At the end of each chapter in your book "All About Lizards", you can include a link to "Gerald's Course On Proper Lizard Care", and make money when people buy it from you.

Secret: People will trust content in a book more than they will on a blog - it's just how it is. Well good for you, because you HAVE books on your blog! More people will click on the links in your book, and more people will buy BECAUSE it was recommended in a book.

91

Make Friends With Other Bloggers

You should already be making friends with other bloggers in the groups we talked about before.

However, there are also a lot of other places you can find bloggers that want to interact, chat, be friends.

The key thing is putting yourself out there.

Comment on other blogs, talk to other bloggers via social networking - add them as friends! Send them an email, get to know them.

You should especially get to know the bloggers who are in the same zone/on the same level as you. You are more likely to interact at a more complete level with people who don't have million dollar blogs, simply because they have more time to talk. But not just time - these people will feel as if YOU can benefit THEM as well, which is completely fine. You should want to help others anyway, so a little cross promotion between you and other bloggers is great!

Also, when you make friends with other bloggers, more people will start to follow you, add you, buy stuff from you - and visit your blog.

There's no doubt that when a blogger who has 3,000 friends has 5 posts on their timeline/page from YOU in the past month, other people will notice. They will add you. They will find out more about you. They will visit your blog! Why? Well, you are friends with THEIR friend, and you are in the same boat (you are a blogger), and obviously they like bloggers - so they'll probably like you!

The more you interact with others, the more good things will happen. You are who you surround yourself with. You don't want to surround yourself with a bunch of people who think change is bad, money is bad, and the internet and technology is bad - you'll NEVER get these people checking out your blog, you'll NEVER influence them to do what you want, you just won't get the interaction you want. But surround yourself with bloggers, with writers, with people who share their knowledge with the world, and you'll have PLENTY of interaction. You'll find more likes on your posts, more shares of your content, more visitors to your blog - you get it, it helps.

If you need a little push to take action - here's an assignment - In the next month, make it so that 50% or MORE of your facebook friends are either bloggers or people DIRECTLY related to your niche or blog topic. You'd be surprised at how much it helps.

92

Capitalizing On Other People's Live Content

This is one of those "out-of-the-box" ideas that no one is doing.

And if you are one of the few that has done this, I'm sorry to let the cat out of the bag.

I call it capitalizing on other people's live content. You've been to a webinar before. You've been to a google hangout. You've at least been to some sort of live event.

Well, where does this live content go once it is finished?

Most of the time, it's lost forever - never gets recorded, never gets posted anywhere. Then sometimes, it just gets posted as a "video replay", but that's about it.

One thing that I have seen NO ONE DO (well, only a few) is transcribe these live events, or write a list of notes ALL ABOUT THE LIVE EVENT.

I don't know, maybe it's just me, but sometimes I feel as if I could have spent my time more wisely by doing something OTHER THAN watching the webinar or live event I've attended. It sucks, but with the amount of live webinars I've been to, it happens - a lot.

So what I've done a few time (and what I believe YOU should do too) is actually spend that time wisely and feel like you are getting something done during these live events that may feel like a waste of time sometimes by TAKING NOTES!

And not just notes so that you can review them later - I'm talking about taking notes and writing your thoughts on someone's live content, then posting it to your blog!!

You get free knowledge and insight from a live event, AND you get an extra piece of content to put on your blog. You can then take the content, spin it, post it elsewhere, share it, then even turn it into your own audios and videos - and re-share!

ANOTHER "SECRET" TIP: You'll find that MANY live events are promoting some type of product or program - and USUALLY these products have AFFILIATE PROGRAMS that you can make money from! So, to add to the benefit of learning something new as well as posting more content to your blog, you can ALSO post affiliate links and make money from the content you post!

I can't believe I shared this with you - but hey, most people will skip this anyway - make sure that person is NOT you! Next time you get invited to a live event or webinar - take notes, post some content, and make some money! And if the webinar or live event isn't promoting a product, you can always promote a product SIMILAR to the content in your notes.

93

People Love Real World Case Studies And Stats

At least I love stats. Don't you? Maybe not stats, but case studies? I just love hearing and reading about other people's success, especially when it is something that is achievable by myself.

When someone wants success in a certain area, they search for answers. They search for other people who have done the same thing. They look for stats, case studies, testimonials.

It doesn't even matter if it's your own testimonial - as long as it tells the story of someone's success, you should include it on your blog!

Search for "[your blog topic] case study" or "[your blog topic] success story" or something similar. You'll find videos, articles, audios, a whole bunch of stuff.

I'd say if you are going to post someone else's case study or success story, only do so in the form of embedding their video on your blog. This just comes down to ethics again - you don't want to repost someone else's written content - it's copyright infringement, and it's FAKE.

If you are going to post written content, make sure it is your OWN success story, your OWN stats, your OWN real life case study.

Your case study can be a review of a product (affiliate promotion, anyone?), a quick post of your stats from a recent campaign or something like that, or even a success story of something that you did that worked out well.

People look for success stories so that they can do the same. But on top of that, people respect you more when they know you've been successful with something. You can promote a product or say how to do something all you want, but if you can't actually show someone that it works or that they can and will benefit from it, then almost all credibility is lost.

Start to post about your successes, your failures, your own case studies, and above all, be real.

94

Write To Help, But Write To SELL

We always talk about value, and of course you are always trying to add value within the content you create. However, if you actually want to make any real money blogging, you have to write to sell.

You don't have to actually sell your own product in order to sell on your blog.

What I'm talking about is changing some of the words in your blog post, and using new words that make people want to take another action with you, whether it is subscribing to you, reading more of your content, watching a video, buying something, joining an email list or club.

Previously, you learned about Call To Actions (CTA). This is BIG with writing to sell.

You don't want to write a post teaching someone how to do something, and then say "have a nice day". NO! Instead, you want to teach them something, and then say "read this other post of mine for more DETAILED INFORMATION", or "subscribe to my email club for extra fun" or "follow me so you don't miss out on more great content!". You can think of other ways to sell your blog, your content, yourself.

You can't expect your audience to be a mind reader. Sometimes you have to TELL them and SELL them on doing something.

If you want them to buy a product, don't just link to it - tell them "click here right now and get the product that helped me achieve everything I wanted and needed".

Now, you don't want every line of your content to be selling something, and you don't want too many CTAs in a single post. But definitely think about writing to sell more. When you write your next blog post, think about what actions you want your readers to take while they read and after they are done. Lead them to the "next step", whatever that may be, and you'll get an increase in general activity on your blog, as well as be able to sell more (your own products, affiliate products, clicks, subscribers, etc.).

95

Blog Aggregation

Blog and content aggregation is becoming more and more of the "norm".

This is one of those things that I would NOT go too crazy with, but use it here and there in the correct way, and you can find some more interaction, and probably a slight increase in visitors (they won't be instant, but they'll be consistent).

Blog aggregation is easy to do, but of course can get time consuming.

Basically, there are "aggregator" websites and services out there that share your blog with the world.

You go to one of these sites (some are free-for-all, some you must register, still free though), and post your blog URL (and alot of the time, your RSS feed URL for your blog), and they aggregator will add your blog and RSS feed to their 'directory' you could call it. These sites essentially push your content out to the world, and give you the chance to get a lot more visitors to your blog.

You may see some direct traffic right away, but the big traffic comes later, when you consistently publish content on your blog. A lot of these aggregation sites will pump your new posts as well, so the more you submit your blog to these sites, and the more content you publish, the more eyes you can get in front of your content.

96

EFFECTIVE DOUBLE VALUE LINK EXCHANGING

Link exchanging is important, double value link exchanging is more important.

So many... so many... so many people are telling you to exchange links. And again, that's where they stop. And then you try it, and then you fail. And then you don't think that strategy works anymore. B.S.

THINGS CHANGE - If you want to stay around, you have to learn how to adapt to the changes that occur online.

Search engines used to ONLY care about the QUANTITY of back links to your blog. You could really just exchange links with like 1,000 websites, and have a full page of links linking to thousands of sites, and have thousands of those sites linking back to you, and Google would rank you #1 for many keywords.

It doesn't work this way anymore.

Search engines caught on, and now we use the term "link farms". Link farms are bad (for the most part). Link farms are those pages that ONLY have links, usually hundreds. In the old days, you'd rank well for lots of these back links, NOW YOU GET PENALIZED.

But have no fear, I have the PERFECT strategy for a VALUE link exchange - in fact, I call it the DOUBLE VALUE LINK EXCHANGE:

So here's how it works... Instead of exchanging links only to be put on a page with a ton of other links, you should INSTEAD make it valuable for both parties by not just exchanging links, but exchanging content!

That's right, it's sort of like a content exchange. The blog content or post doesn't need to be long - although it can be if you want. 100 or 200 words will do. Then, add the link to the end of the blog post.

This type of link exchange is valuable because not only are both of you getting a back link with the anchor text as your keyword, but you are ALSO getting to add keywords and content on and around your link(s), which allows search engines to pick up your link easier, and more than likely they will rank you better because there is actually more content that goes with the link - and as search engines have shown, content is king.

The next time you or someone else goes to do a link exchange, tell them about this idea. Your post doesn't have to be anything spectacular - it can even be a short tip, then a sentence or two saying what your blog is about, then your link, then one or two sentence outro or CTA. Easy to create, not a lot of time taken out of your day, and it benefits both you AND the other person. So there you have it, effective double value link exchanging. Use this today!

97

Keep Some Content Protected

Ever think of running a membership blog?

I'm not saying you should restrict EVERYONE from reading your blog posts. I'm not even saying you should restrict all your blog posts in general.

However, one strategy you can use is restricting and protecting SOME of your content.

Now, this is more of an advanced strategy, so if you haven't implemented the other strategies and tips in this book, do those first. Then once you've got the hang of your blog, you can implement this strategy and get a lot more out of your blog.

The reason this is a bit complicated is because you'll have to install some sort of membership plug-in into your blog. Some are free, some are paid. Right now WishList Member is what most people I know are going for - easy to use, LOTS of options and customization.

Here's what you can do with this: Keep 80% or 90% of your content free to read, free to share. Then, PROTECT the other small percentage of your content. I would say to not protect articles only - protect the POWERFUL, SUPER-VALUABLE content - the longer in-depth videos, the free e-book downloads, the advanced training, maybe a 'members only podcast'.

Membership/access to your protected content can either be paid for OR be given for free - but someone MUST register and become a member in order to view this content.

How does this help?

Well, first and foremost, you create a sense of exclusivity, a sense that "what you get for free isn't EVERYTHING I have to offer". You make people want more - so they join you in order to get it.

Also, once these people join/become a member, YOU NOW HAVE THEIR EMAIL ADDRESS. You shouldn't spam them (that's illegal and unethical), but you can definitely send a "broadcast" to these people telling them about new member content, as well as new products you launch.

The people who give you their email address in order to join your exclusive area on your blog are taking that next step with you, which provides a much higher chance that these people will take even further steps with you.

Put it this way - You can't expect to say "buy this now" right away, and have every person whipping out their credit card. But, lead them in the right direction over time, and they'll get there.

Post something on social media, and get people to your blog. Then they read some posts. Then they download a free e-book. Then they find out they can get more free e-books by joining the exclusive members area of your blog, so they join. Later you launch more e-books for free, and they download those as well (and you'll probably make some money if you are promoting an affiliate product in these e-books). Then, after you gain all of this credibility, you launch a course, a product, a book, an audio series, a coaching program, a paid membership site - and you SELL IT TO THEM. Instead of getting a 0.005% buy rate, you could be looking at a 1%, 2%, even 5% buy rate, because people TRUST you and LIKE you.

98

Syndicate Blogging Gets Bigger

Blog syndication, what a wonderful promotion strategy.

Blog syndication (at least the type that I'm talking about) works like this: You post content to your blog. You copy and paste that content into a blog syndication service. This service republishes your content with the hopes that people will find it on their syndication site and then go check out your other blog posts on your blog.

This works similar to aggregation, but although they are similar, the structure and features of the site are different.

With aggregation, your blog as a whole gets added to a type of directory that allows people to find your blog easier.

With blog syndication, it's also about making your blog easier to find, but isn't just about submitting your blog as a whole. Usually with most syndication sites, you actually post your CONTENT to these sites. They republish your content, and put it into a category and sub-category so that others looking for something on a specific topic can find your blog post.

Syndication allows your content to be found and shared by more people. It can also give you a hell of a lot of back links - and as you know, back links are KEY for blogging success.

You don't have to syndicate all of your blogs posts, but you should get in the habit of syndication. It only helps, especially if you find that your blog isn't being seen by as many people as you want.

99

AUTOMATE AS MUCH AS YOU POSSIBLY CAN

AUTOMATION IS THE KEY TO SUCCESS.

Seriously, nothing is better than automating most of your daily processes. When you can automate 90% of your blogging business, it makes it that much easier to only work on the things that will make your blog more successful.

Trust me, I know I covered a lot in this book, and I don't expect you to do everything at once! But one thing I made sure to do was give you insight and direction on how to automate tasks on your blog so that you only have to do them once, and they'll continue to benefit you and your blog.

If there is something that will benefit your blog forever that you only have to set up ONCE, then DO IT! Always be looking out for software, plug-ins, websites, and services that make blogging easier and more care-free.

You bought this book because you love blogging - it shouldn't be a chore. That's why it's always nice to automate things, so you can focus on the FUN STUFF.

Defining your mission and goals from the start is an automated task. Once it's done, it's there, and it's there forever - you don't have to do another damn thing about it! Submit your RSS feed to directories, and every time you post a new piece of content, these directories will pick up on it and post it. Go find a social media tool (right now I use HootSuite), and instead of having to manually share your blog posts on 10 or 20 different social networks and streams, you can just hit 1 button to share it with as many of your own social streams as you want. Set up that guest-blogger page, never touch it again and get extra valuable content. Add the "value link exchange" page, and get requests to add your link to THEIR site.

The more you automate, the more successful your blog gets. Automation gives your blog constant momentum, and allows your blog to grow to the heights you dream of. And when you add different forms of optimization, sharing/return visitors, and monetization, you can make some good passive and residual income from your blog as well.

BONUS

Beyond Blogging

I wanted to take a few minutes to tell you probably the MOST important message and info you will get from this book.

The point of this bonus section/chapter/tip is to get you in the mindset that your blog can be taken to much bigger levels and new heights.

Don't just think of your blog as a content-hub, that's what Squidoo and Hubpages and article directories are for. Your blog is a business, your blog is YOU.

What do you want to do in life? What are your motives, your goals, your dreams? Do you want to write 500 word articles for the rest of your life, or are you in this for something bigger?

Start thinking about branding, start thinking about products, start thinking about other ways you can enrich and add value to other people's lives through your own content, through YOUR message.

Don't think of your blog visitors as traffic, think of them as a movement.

Don't make a product on your blog just for the sake of making money from it. Enrich other people's lives with your product, and make your product so good that people begin to want ANYTHING and EVERYTHING you have to offer.

Essentially, you are filling the gaps that people need filled.

If you want to motivate people, your goal should be to get people to your blog who want to be motivated. From there, your goal is to get them to become a repeat visitor. This can be down through social media, email lists, membership sites, a book that links back to your blog, subscribing to your YouTube account or video channel, etc.

Basically, you want the fun to go on as long as you can.

Always be searching for ways to collect info from your visitors. An email list is the perfect way to do this. Give your visitors a free gift for subscribing to your email list, then add tons of value into their lives through the content you send in your emails, and get your audience to trust you and love you.

Nothing beats trust and credibility.

When you are able to build your lists, your subscribers, your members, and your visitors to great heights, and assuming you are doing everything you can to help your audience, there's absolutely NO LIMITATIONS as to what you can do.

When you create a product, you'll have 100,000 people to tell about it. When you post a video, it will be shared immediately, and possibly go viral. When you start a new affiliate program, people will promote your product, and both they AND you will make money.

You can do it, I know you can. It all comes down to hard work in the beginning, as well as the creation of automated systems, interaction with your audience, value-adding and life-enriching content, and massive, massive action.

I truly hope you got everything you wanted out of this book. I know that when you follow these tips and strategies, you'll see your blog moving higher in the rankings, you'll see your visitor count rise as well, and you'll see money in your bank account, possibly for the first time ever from your online business and blog.

The first step is obviously taking action right now. Pick the 10 easiest or most-fun sounding tips and strategies, and do those 10 before you go to bed. Then, continue adding strategies, tips, and automated systems to your blogging efforts, and before you know it, your blog will be 10 times or 100 times the blog it is right now. IT'S ACTION TIME! GO GO GO!

THANKS FOR READING!

Thanks so much for reading. Again, my goal in this book is to give you everything I possibly can in order to make your blog successful, but even more so to make YOU successful.

I love blogging, and I love bloggers - but as you already know, there's so much crap out there, and so many varying strategies and people telling you what you should do.

I'm not saying you MUST follow every tip in this book, but I can guarantee you that if you did, your blog will only increase in size.

Please don't be the person that says "cool book" and then keeps doing what you're doing now. If you aren't as successful as you want to be right now, the only thing you need to do is make a change.

I know it's sometimes difficult when you get thrown a ton of information at you. You don't have to do this all at once - think of this book as an arsenal of blogging tips and strategies that you can use now AND in the future. Whenever you have some time on your hands, or whenever you feel like your blog needs a push, come back to this book and implement some more strategies!

Keep adding value into people's lives, keep working hard, and above all, KEEP TAKING ACTION, EVERY DAY.

www.ingramcontent.com/pod-product-compliance
Lightning Source LLC
Chambersburg PA
CBHW071758200526
45167CB00017B/412

* 9 7 8 1 5 0 3 2 2 9 2 6 6 *